THE NEXT OF US IS ABOUT
TO BE BORN

The Next of Us Is About to Be Born

The Wick Poetry Series Anthology

In Celebration of the Twenty-fifth Anniversary

of the Wick Poetry Center

Edited by Maggie Anderson

The Kent State University Press

Kent, Ohio

© 2009 by The Kent State University Press, Kent, Ohio 44242

ALL RIGHTS RESERVED

Library of Congress Catalog Card Number 2008043866

ISBN 978-1-60635-021-8

Manufactured in the United States of America

LIBRARY OF CONGRESS CATALOGING-IN-PUBLICATION DATA

The next of us is about to be born / edited by Maggie Anderson.

    p.   cm.

Includes the work of 55 poets who have published chapbooks or first books in the Wick poetry series of the Kent State University Press.

ISBN 978-1-60635-021-8 (pbk. : alk. paper) ∞

1. American poetry—20th century. 2. American poetry—21st century.

I. Anderson, Maggie. II. Wick poetry series.

PS615.N49 2009

811'.5408—dc22   2008043866

British Library Cataloging-in-Publication data are available.

13 12 11 10 09   5 4 3 2 1

CONTENTS

The Next of Us Is About to Be Born includes the work of fifty-five poets who have published chapbooks or first books in the Wick Poetry Series of the Kent State University Press. Most of these poets published their *first* work through the Wick Poetry Series. As the Wick Poetry Center celebrates its twenty-fifth year of encouraging new voices, it seems fitting to acknowledge with this anthology the crucial part that the book series has played in all the activities of the Wick Poetry Center and the important first step this series has provided for new and emerging poets of all ages from Ohio and nationally.

The Wick Poetry Series is only one of the several projects of the Wick Poetry Center. Founded in 1984 by Robert and Walter Wick in memory of their sons Stan (1962–80) and Tom (1956–73), the Center's mission has grown from a single scholarship program to promoting opportunities for emerging and established poets and poetry audiences locally, regionally, and nationally. This now takes the form of scholarships, internships, and graduate fellowships; a regional program of poetry outreach in schools and community centers; a nationally recognized reading series; and, of course, the Wick Poetry Series of chapbooks and first books of poetry.

All books in the Wick Poetry Series are chosen through competitions. The Chapbook series is open to Ohio writers, and is divided into a Student Competition and an Open Competition. As the editor of the Chapbook series, I choose the winning manuscripts from both competitions. The national Stan and Tom Wick Poetry Prize for a first book of poetry began in 1993, and its winners are selected each year by a noted poet; among the judges we have been honored to have are Lucille Clifton, Marilyn Hacker, Philip Levine, Alberto Ríos, Gerald Stern, C. K. Williams, and Eleanor Wilner. (For all competitions, finalists are first identified by screeners who are published poets unaffiliated with Ohio or Kent State University.)

The work of the poets represented here shows them at the very beginning of what has become, for many, a successful career in publishing, teaching, and the literary arts. They have gone on to win numerous awards, to publish two or three or even four books (often in several genres), and they remain connected to the many activities of the Wick Poetry Center and to the Kent State University Press, which brought their earliest poems into print.

In selecting the poems for this anthology, I was reminded of how consistently good the work is, even though several of the poets were undergraduate students when their work was selected. There is, perhaps, some tonal or subject similarity—for example, since the Chapbook series is for Ohio poets, there are a number of Ohio landscapes reflected in the poems. Yet these are well balanced by other chapbooks and by the voices of the First Book poets, whose work contains scenes and themes both national and international. While the notes on contributors at the back of this book will tell you which competition the poets won and who selected the book, one thing is clear: whatever their age or publication record at the time, all of these poets demonstrate the boldness, confidence, and originality that often characterizes the work of new writers.

As I write this, the 2008 First Book manuscript has just arrived. The judge this year was Stephen Dunn, who selected a book entitled *The Infirmary* by Edward Micus, a poet from North Mankato, Minnesota. I have the sense of anticipation I always feel with a new manuscript in hand—and the joy that editing this series provides me: a chance to welcome another new voice into our poetry. I think of Rosemary Willey's line, which coincidentally ends this anthology and appropriately provides

its title: "the next of us is about to be born."

> Maggie Anderson
> Director, Wick Poetry Center
> Editor, Wick Poetry Series
> Kent, Ohio, 2008

ACKNOWLEDGMENTS

This anthology, and in fact the whole Wick Poetry Series, owes much to the support and collaboration of the Kent State University Press. I am grateful to former director John Hubbell, who saw the value and vision in this series at the very beginning, and to Will Underwood, the current director, who has supported the series for more than fifteen years. Special thanks are due to the KSU Press staff past and present, especially Joanna Craig and Mary Young in editorial, Brett Neff and Susan Cash in marketing, and Christine Brooks and Darryl Crosby in design. Thanks to their creativity and skill, the Wick Poetry Series is known for books that are not only well-written but beautifully produced. For invaluable assistance with editorial matters as well as with manuscript preparation, I heartily thank Robin Bellinson, doctoral candidate in the Kent State University Department of English and graduate assistant for the Northeast Ohio MFA in creative writing. Robin served as the editorial assistant for this anthology, and I am grateful for her energy, skill, persistence, and sharp editorial eye.

    I also want to thank Kent State University Trustees Professor Paul Gaston and his wife Eileen for their support of the Wick Poetry Center through the creations of the Wick Poetry Corner in the Kent State University Main Library and the Tyler Lee Gaston Collection of twentieth- and twenty-first-century poetry, endowed in memory of their son Tyler Lee Gaston (1980–2004). Finally, without the ongoing generosity and vision of Robert and Walter Wick and their families, the Wick Poetry Center would not exist. Although, as Robert has written, the Center came about "out of painful beginnings," it has grown over the last twenty-five years to be a program of rich opportunity, providing many joyful beginnings for poets from Ohio and throughout the country. All royalties from the sale of this book will go to the Wick Poetry Center for continued support of Wick Poetry Series projects.

M.A.

BLUE

The house is blue, milky and narcotic. The round shingles like petals, a million of them, like a field of glossy oysters with their prize bellies, like chaste lace on the girl's cuff. The trim mother called *gingerbread* haunting the windows, as if carpenters were elves, and the thin scroll of oak could melt in your mouth, spice burning the tongue. The air is thick with hyacinth and lilac, spathes of barbiturate and kiss. The long necks of delphinium with their bells like tiny mouths, tiny veins of forget-me-nots crawling across the slated path, the single scrape of geranium. The back door cracks open like a robin's egg, glossy skin of membrane still clinging. A wool slipper drowns in a pool of yolk. The tiny nest is empty—the bird died, its feathers still wet and leafy lanugo. It slept in the porcelain bowl warmed in the oven. There is no song, just a calico dress and the beat of the girl's heart as she eats her porridge. Her spoon is open like a cyclops looking. It is searching the bottom like a hand reading the floor of the pond. She stays down there a long time. She works hard. She works until her face glows like a halo, cyanotic. Her eyes pearl and gleam. She is not a mechanic, she is a machine. She is the switch flicked on, the *go*. Oh yes, she can swim now. In the blue water, she is a swan. And there is a promise. A promise circling like a wing inside her.

1

Needle to thread. Scythe to wheat. Foot to pedal. Hammer and sickle. *Work, work, work.* She has three sisters. At dusk she drinks tea. From the silver belly of a samovar. In the dark she drinks vodka. She takes a lover who smells of fresh meat and the pines. The hunt is on him, like his tongue on the crest of her sex. Like the little forest of white down on her breasts. On the nape of her neck. A hunger grows. Grows inside her. *Note: She is not hungry for him. He is a symptom of that hunger. An empty cup she could keep replenishing. A clue: bread crust, apple core, chicken bone.* Wish-bone. *Knowing three languages is a useless luxury in this town. A sort of unwanted appendage. A sixth finger.* She can't remember the Italian for *window.* She climbs the ceilings. The water spouts. She eats strawberries, using her lips like a blind girl uses her fingers. Little match girl. Little lamb. Little shoe. Black boot. *Achoo.* A little red wine? Red Riding Hood. All the better to see you with. To read you with, my dear. *Follow.* Over the river. Through the woods. To the sea. Knees deep in the salty water. To the island of Crete. To Tunis. To Florence. To Russia. To Moscow. Finally. *Finally,* you say, to Moscow. She will arrive on that page. That splendid stage of trajectory. Of destiny. Destination. She is splendid. Sexy. *Oh baby.* She is Little Miss Adjective. She will wear her best black dress. Sings a soft song when she walks. Syllables of silk, of organza and tulle say *Hush, we are almost at "The End."* She wears a veil of Swiss lace. *Real,* they said about the lace she was wearing. Little accents, little umlauts, tiny apostrophes like snowflakes sting her cheeks. She does not blush. She makes the sign of the cross. She makes a date. With hunger. With the great black cloak of a train. But this time she doesn't lie down. She refuses to make her bed. To spill her blood like children. She doesn't set herself on fire. She won't sign her name or spell you her secrets. She won't uncross her legs. She opens her mouth instead. She opens her mouth and she. She eats. She eats it all: *porters, nannies with babies, the tracks, the coal, the iron, the ore.* She dines for pages, for chapters. Eating paper, drinking the sweet black ink, wiping her mouth on her sleeve. Then she eats her best black dress and so she is naked. And so she is huge. And it is you, it is you she is holding like an open book, well loved, in her hands.

This is a quiet grave. It is not made of myths, of great barbarous fish, of coral, or salt. No one submerges himself with metal and rubber, no one shines her white light along the floor. Search parties have been suspended. There is no treasure buried here. This is the place of what-is-not. Of a green so green those flying above it would call it blue. Of a black so black it glows. This is a world with its own species of ghosts—plankton drifting inside her, the barnacles nesting on her hips, her wrists, their whole beings mouths frozen in horror. Sound turned into silence—like cloth on the floor is the shed skin of the lover. Like sheets bereft of the shapes that slept. Once upon a time, she was all escape—her long hair, siren of copper and cinnamon, burning a comet behind her. Her long legs loved heels and short skirts, craved the hard slap of the city beneath her. You would have read this girl. You both wanted more. But she doesn't remember how she got here, in this bed that consumed her. Why she can't put her lipstick on, why one would press color like a promise to the lips. It must have begun with red. But the beginning of this story is lost to the water, you could rake its bottom of leaves and sticks like tea, you could spear one of its last trout and study the slick pages of its intestine. The girl is leagues and leagues away from the first kiss of prologue, but she, throat caked with mud, white skin scaled verdigris, must be the message within the bottle. Words grow in her belly. It doesn't matter who put them there. If they are the children of plankton, descendants of eels and pond scum. They come to her as twins, triplets, and septuplets, whole alphabets swimming inside her. Each one is a bubble, a bread crumb, a rung to climb to the top. And as she ascends she names them with names cradled inside her. Her feet kick and her arms clutch. Her body strong and slippery, a great tongue that propels her: *A is for apple, B is for bone, for boat, C is for candle, for cunt, for cut.*

3

WHAT THE DEAD SEE

after Frank Stanford

Back then I never let on. Besides, no one was there to set the record straight, the womb we fell from, soused with liquor. And there was any kind of excuse. I was younger than I ever knew, in air swimming with insects. Sometimes, talking with the Baptist preacher on the patio about the folks who have gone from this world, I felt them, like they were fish bones caught in my throat. *The dead have things,* he'd say, *they don't even let on to the devil they know. The living does too.* Like my head was a transistor radio, he wanted to find that gospel station, make me fear the Lord. His breath, warm on my face, a whiff of fish thawing, the rain like small feet on the lake. I'd watch it and sip from a green Coca-cola bottle slow, wondering what the Lord and devil don't know, seeing nobody seeing us. Nights, when my folks came home late, the headlights crossed my ceiling. Shadows kept falling and falling. I'd watch my sister's boyfriend slip out. She was good at faking shit, like sleep, like caring what she did. Afterwards, I'd listen. Sometimes the dark would look at itself and sigh, and the wind would blow in the alfalfa field. I'd hear someone whispering so soft, no one heard her words.

It was Indian summer, after a change in weather brought the bees inside, when Grandma moved in. Jimmy, the farmhand, and I were sitting by the silo, waiting for the milk truck when she stepped out of a yellow cab, wearing a fur muff and a red satin cap. That afternoon when the sun burned through the mist, bees were crawling up the windows looking for holes in the screens. Before my mom could get a grip on her, Grandma had hosed every bug in our house down with Raid and taken over doing the laundry too. If there was a thing Grandma liked, it was clean clothes. And other things were dead bugs and the Lord, Jesus Christ. But she didn't want to be bothered with the clothes dryer. She liked our clothes hung outside, saying the Lord liked honest work, which meant something you did without a socket.

It rained so much that fall, all our lettuce got slugs and the wilt. My mom said the sheets mildewed. After my grandma took the linens in from the line, they were damp and crawling with daddy longlegs. Mom would slip them in the dryer, whining under her breath about how Grandma had her ways of dipping into everybody's affairs like a pumpkin vine in compost.

Nights, while Grandma read me her favorite parts of the Bible, mostly about Jesus performing the miracles, I'd sweep my sheets with my fingers, feeling for bug legs. I never could figure how any insect could walk on those legs, thin and wispy as hairs.

It was a day like any other day.
I'd been down at the pond,
catching crawdads in a bucket,
watching a chicken hawk
circle overhead.
Grandma Lou was in the orchard
picking fruit.
For lunch my mother served cold biscuits
and stew.
Grandma Lou told us then she'd been out
gathering the pickling pears
when it happened.
The voice of God came through.
Lou, it said, *I'm calling home my faithful servant,*
old Grandma Mason.
She looked up at the naked air,
and saw the angels flocking like crows,
though to tell it honest,
she said, she could hardly see
for the light blazing.
Mark my words, Grandma Lou sighed,
forking out another heap of tomato beef stew.
Miz Mason won't be long for this world.

Dad kept chewing his food.
My mother picked a daddy longlegs
off the magnolia blossom
and carried it outside.
No one paid Grandma much heed.
She always had a way
of forecasting doom,
knowing just who was dying
which week.
Said she could feel 'em
like a minnow
slipping between her palms.

A day or two after Miz Mason passed on,
Grandma Lou and I sat out on the porch
shucking corn and picking off earworms.

I asked her did she recollect
what the angels wore,
and if they played harps or dulcimers
like my mother did.
But Grandma Lou said it looked like
she wasn't one
to see God's minions up close,
but it must be gobs of them up there,
sort of like bees on the moon.

DIRTY SOCKS, 11:30 P.M.

Because I am alone
and raising children,
I'm standing in the kitchen
sniffing my daughter's socks
trying to decide whether to
wash them and then use all that
electricity for the drier
so they'll be dry in the morning,
or whether to let her wear
dirty socks a second day.

8

This matters because it isn't
ecological to run the drier
for a pair of little socks,
but it certainly is not good
to let one's kindergartner
wear socks a second day
when they're dirty
and smelly.
You're not like this.
Your children have lots of socks
in their drawers that they like to wear.

My daughter has lots of socks
in her drawer, but she only likes
to wear certain ones.
I'm confused by all of this.
I haven't said divorce is worse than death.
I've only said my daughter, now,
for the first time in her life,
is having a terrible time finding
just the right socks.
Sometimes she cries over this.
Sometimes she will not let me hold her.
Sometimes she's frantic about her socks
and I sit on the edge of her bed
wanting fiercely to hold her,
and she will not let me.

THROUGH ALL THIS

My daughter wants to know
if it's okay to cry out loud.
I've watched her practice
biting her teeth together
to keep the sounds from coming out.
They're so embarrassing,
now that she's in kindergarten.

Yes, I tell her. *Cry loudly.*
Let's practice.
Sitting together on my bed,
I show her how I cry with lots of noise.
She laughs and says do it again,
and I do it again,
more pitifully than before.
Her laughing is jubilant.
It's okay to cry out loud, I tell her.
I do it all the time, I tell her.

The next morning
she says she thinks she's going to cry
when I leave her at her baby-sitter's.
She doesn't want to eat the carrots
I've packed in her little lunch,
and today I tell her that, too, is okay.
But when it comes time for me to leave,
she doesn't make noise.
She does that quiet thing she's learned to do
now that she's big.

Joys Impregnate, Sorrows Bring Forth
—William Blake, "The Marriage of Heaven and Hell"

When love stops for some reason,
my language makes sense for a while.
I understand all that surrounds this.
I can explain the thread count of cotton sheets,
the warmth of skin, the candle on the table,
the glass of water. Even the sky outside the windows
above the headboard can be explained.

But I cannot explain the midpoint
of what has happened here,
the falling place.
I try animal howlings,
delirious, on my hands and knees,
my forehead pressed to the kitchen floor.
I get familiar with the tiles in the bathroom.
I laugh, take long baths, eat ice cream, cry.
Drink a little coffee, tea, wine.
I sit in the corners of unlikely rooms
rocking like a stunned child.

Grief matters.
It materializes each sound and movement
into sticks laid straight.
A voice says, *Your hair wants cutting.*
I cut it. It's long enough to braid;
my sorrowing, stupefied fingers weave
together the raft that is ferrying me
across the black tongue river
into the very mouth of darkness.
I keep going.

NOTES FOR A NARRATIVE

1. in cleavage and fear of the dark of the second-grade school desk rests his mother's photograph 2. loss, perfume of soft Saturday evenings, mouth moist with attended love 3. and a voice a soprano note held and yearning to slip into palms, pulse next to him in pew 4. in pew her voice ringing down the spine welling its drift from a choir loft 5. or, climbing the stairs clutching her side for cramps she feels the months fall and rest to be studied in the bathroom light 6. there is drama played out in the strain in passion he can't see 7. indifference to the weight of groceries lifted in each Saturday hands numb from lifting, listing 8. small drama of frozen foods, odor of onions in brown paper bags—small gratitudes in mesh—the cans and cans of Cragmont Cola—9. there is a resistant tendon 10. an arthritic shoulder howls beneath his touch 11. my mother told me a story

11

We're driving. *Chatterbox, we're running out of room.*

The lean-to of abandoned America throws a shadow
     toward the middle.
Everybody run
at the edge of gilt. Do you see how a house

nearly fallen can mimic

the hopeless slope of the land itself?
Weeds entwine the doormats of the country. No entering
here. "Ruins provide the incentive for restoration,

a return to origins." Let's fill up.

"That is how we reproduce the cosmic scheme and
     correct history."
I'm ravenous. That old New Church
tilts at the center

of the land, curl, palm

of land. That house there
needs a shave. There's a bed of trees holding up a wall
the whole world raging around it.

In Whatsville, an empty trailer's

the kind of kid no one played with anyway.
Where light can penetrate
a window a canvas of

fresh gold leaf hangs. *Don't touch it, it's unreal*

at the center. In Jerksville, leaves blow through walls.
Finally, a group of large men in bright orange vests
lift a washing machine from the side of the road:

rainwater streamed from its sides into sunlight,

some kinda weird appreciation. Let go. Closed door on
    closed door.
The lean-to of abandoned America offers no outlet.
I'm feeling real stuffy, like I can't breathe.

Doors hang on hinges, arguments too bored to continue.

World keeps spinning.
Do you see how that house there though empty can't help
but say   . *Wind's too loud,*

I can't hear. What's up ahead?

Ahead is another center of a house turned
inside-out. The elements play rudely, heeding no privacy.   13
Letters scatter to the corners,

wish you were here, stay put

'*cause I'm coming.*
This range and hill and those trees
will eat right through all of this.

CHAOS

This is the New Science
        a Post-Modern Science
 an Anti-Science
            against Newton against Method
        against the flawed Ideal

This is a science Heisenberg
        (if he were here)
        would love
 a science of wayward atoms
            unscheduled hurricanes
 of volcanic eruptions
                earthquakes
                that never take place
        when expected

This is a Quiet Science
        ruled by the unseen
            and unmeasurable
 blessed by subversions
                terrorists of order
 infinite anti-patterns
            the curl of
 smoke
                the unpredictable tangles
        of capillaries and roots
            and branches
                of snowflakes

THANKSGIVING

In Madrid, around midnight, Julie and I,
half-undressed in maddening heat, passed
midway between blue-and-white-tiled bath
and twin beds, when just-like-that the lights
went out and we stopped in the blackened kiln
of our room, fearing Basques dynamiting
power stations and surly Franco-ites'
threats to restore order to the land.

When have I ever had reason to fear?
In that blackened room we listened—sirens
wailed many blocks away and all I could
think was to tiptoe over and re-check
the lock. Then we sat huddling together,
our chicken hearts pounding for an hour,
shuddering over nothing in the dark.
Who has had reason to fear? My Uncle Jim,

United States Air Force Colonel, professional
navigator and bombardier, who claimed
to flatten Cambodian villages
with the same feeling as when he exterminated
random ant hills in the rectangular
and oval rose gardens by his garage.
Now, I think of his fears—small-arms fire
from the ground, an occasional rocket

or anti-aircraft burst, his wife and kids
safe asleep in their suburb; and I think
of all the families huddled inside huts
in their guerilla villages, fleeing
each time the awesome birds swooped to drop
black eggs that burst in deadly madness;
and I think of my father, who did his
military stint during peacetime, how he

threatened to take Jim outside and beat him
for every single fucking bomb he dropped—
and all this during Thanksgiving dinner,
1972, in front of my mother's

entire extended family. I was eleven
at the time, but I understood
fear and hate and why my mom kept crying
all the long quiet ride home from grandma's.

Monday, like the unconscious Sunday
before it, lies drunk on wind
and blinding sun. It rusts in memories
of wet city streets and gutters
flooded with the thick flow
of blood and barefoot children
chasing down cracked sidewalks
lofting burnt-out light bulbs
onto rough asphalt, relishing
the explosions of thin glass.
The children's ears, numbed by shouts,
feign deafness, ignore cries
of why, why can't you be quiet,
don't you know your father
is asleep, don't you know
he'll whip you if you wake him?

At noon, the children stand outside
the bathroom door and watch their father's
distant face blur in the mirror
as the blade, dull-edged, scrapes
graying whiskers from chin and neck.
They hope each shaky stroke
tempts a repentance in blood
for days gone unremembered.

Little boys bored with Sunday rip pages
by the handful from handout Bibles, curse
the New Testament and don't believe
in anything that can't be seen. They laugh
at abstractions like a good family life
and love. They've seen what's real:
a father passed out each morning
naked on the couch, violent at the rise
of sound. On these sunny Mondays that lie
unconscious of past Sundays, children run
berserk through city streets, drunk
on wind and sunshine, destroying anything
that isn't blue.

BIRCH CANOE
   for Lieutenant Dan Suttles

After supper, my daughter asked me,
Any bad stuff today?

I would like to answer *no,*
but she's seen the six o'clock news
yellow tape surrounding the trailer's shell,
the story of sisters playing with matches
our fire captain, tired, begging parents
to put lighters up, install smoke alarms.

She knows the child named Sara
came to my hospital.
I am touched by her concern,
Will they make it, Mom?

I try to tell her about the fireman,
young and sweaty and mustached,
his scorched suit
kneeling beside our gurney,
holding swollen sooty fingers
of a toddler he did not know,
praying for this flower he'd gone
into the flames to gather.

I try to tell her
about men who are gentle and strong,
men who rise without hesitation,
become larger than themselves
and do not paint their faces
with arrows and do not thump
their chests blue.

I do not know
how they tell themselves not to be afraid,
how they let the black smoke

swallow them
over and over.

I just know tonight
this fireman was a birch canoe;
he swam into the fire
and pulled Sara back
into this world,
that is never easy.

FOR MAUDE CALLEN: NURSE MIDWIFE, PINEVILLE, NC, 1951

I speak of a woman, blue black midwife
Of April fog, flood, swamp, and July nights
When Maude Callen's hands layered newsprint
In circles as a weaver works her loom,
Slow, to catch blood straw, placenta, save sheets.
I sing kitchen lamplight, clean cloths, Lysol,
Cord ties, gloves, gown and mask; she readies
For this crowning, first mother, purple cries.
I sing of sweat and gush and tear, open thighs
And triangle moons, ringlets, charcoal hair.
I sing sixteen-hour days, Maude's tires bare.
Mud country roads, no man doctor for miles.
I sing transition, collapse of mountains,
Crimson alluvium, the son untangled.

BUTTERFLY

The thing I keep thinking is these young men
are much too weak to make love.
These boys with yellow hair and blue tattoos
and bristly mustaches who are married
and dying with AIDS cannot enter each other
in the old way—bony hips hang,
unbeautiful, too tired to pump.

Like soft cow bells their hoop earrings
tinkle in ER, room thirteen,
as they press cool cloths to foreheads,
pass tissues for sticky green phlegm.
They wait for the doctor and lab techs
and nurses who mark their plastic name bands
with a *B*. *B* for *blood hazard*. *B* for *boys*.
B for *bad*. Orange-ball stickers tag
their charts; flags go up that say danger.

I am their nurse, and when they ask
for blankets, they cover each other the way
I spread quilts on my daughter in her crib.

They are half of a butterfly on gray cement;
their skin shrinks and tarnishes,
bodies cave in, revival tents
collapsing the final week of summer.

They cough as I enter their room,
and something in me stiffens.
Even this far away in my mask and gown
and gloves trying hard to say—*I care
that you suffer, that your cottage burns—
its flames reach inside my tent*. Whatever
chokes in this fire is large and soundless and pale.

I keep thinking as these men lift each others'
heads from pillow, gently tilt straws
close to dusky lips, hold hands as needles
dig for veins and pull and straighten
hospital sheets hour after wounded hour—
they are migrating back to the cocoon,
the place where brown masks
protect the unbeautiful.

PULLED DOWN

We came from Pickett—land down under the mountain.
We left our houses empty and shuttered with light.
For three days to the brick yards at Robbins,
another to the new shaft above Glenmary,
our wagons swung like the windy fields we left.
The wages we came for we called *public works.*
And some men were lucky, worked near the entrance, the good air,
some in the mill that razed unblemished timber,
but others each day in the shaft rooms
broke and sent out the coal that sealed them in.
A man who brought bad news came home, bathed twice,
saying *I can't go as I am.* Women
bent among their staked vines in gardens;
our Mason's emblem praised the strong right arm.
And we had peacocks in our yards for something pretty
and the foreman's daughter in her pretty fat.
When our companies left, we pulled down company houses
and built other houses from them, which have fallen,
and The Hundreds, and the tipple, and coke ovens,
so many names to tell you for gone things.
The Hiwassi Land Company has planted it all in pine
and sprayed the oaks so they died standing
and stand, a peeled, monumental white
unlike our land: green stroke that hooks, pulls down.

LIKELY

Magnolia bloom can sex the air
until one thinks for long blanknesses
only *magnolia, magnolia.*
The tree shakes with the climbing of two girls.
The taller, stretched among four branches
looks up, carrying a knife.
The other settles at a lesser place
and thinks of falling. Magnolia
withers if touched. The petals
spot where the fingers were, then darken,
spoiling the smell. A girl raised
to be her daddy's boy knows to reach,
slowing and slowing the hand until
it wavers with the flower.
She cuts the slight wood at the stem,
tips to her a color of things hidden—
skin at the lifted clothes, or the shining
averted face of a woman undressing.
The younger girl will run alongside with the news.
The flower floats all night in a glass,
the kitchen lit in other places by the moon.

23

THE CICADAS

Of constant things, they are most constant,
inciting memory, never the thing remembered
but the attendant, bordering the way into memory,
girls strewing petals the day of the wedding

within veils of wings. Hear the pattern to the confusion:
something fumbled for, and dropped, and fumbled for,
the right bead slipped on a string. A thread apparent,
a limb. The summer night is always dimmed

by the woman in her slip at the window,
car headlights on the dark stain of the river
that extinguish, and other light scattered on the river
the way memory obstructs a certain dark—

The ring of children has scattered. They hide
and glitter, small lungs spreading, folding.
Already the first call back *safe! home!*
Now you can bear to remember what you

could bear to do once, carried by breathing
so like this music, in which what you lose, recurs.
The scale of the night slowly fills with petals,
leaves edged in weak light, the laboring wings.

WAKING OR SLEEPING

You sleep to feel the weight: ten thousand pounds
of ivy under the trees, olive greens, susurrations
of vein and bind inside the eyes.

That Steller's jay now caught in the mouth
of the oak is a type of sleep. A type of drink,
to see and scream on pyracantha wine

a neighbor listening. The black braille of asphalt
remembers. It cracks. It reads you back, each step.
It reads the feel of feet like so much skin, routine.   25

Like so much sun. Gasoline, geranium, semen, mint.
In the white arms of laundry you smell nobody
home. You sleep to touch the body already gone.

SUCCESS

Of course it's an old paradox, and that's how we earn it,
one step in the right direction counterveiled by lust.

I go to a lecture on Keats. He is still dying in the eye
of his twenty-fifth birthday. Then a friend arrives

from out of state to say she is no longer alone, that success
in her case is a nine-month sentence, a line that is moving

to swell out her frame into an unwanted name. Or a student,
not quite a friend, who years ago in the shadow

of a great loss tattooed her skin with a ribbon of witness,
who now stands in my office on the brink of another

friendship to tell me she is positive, how things line up
with other things, the meticulous darkness of blood.

Lust is one word for devouring, success an evening of
the score. Warranty, return address, what is ever covered

except rest? All disclosures are beautiful. All disclosures
add up points with beautiful futility. The trail of waking's

a complicated dream. *Half in love with easeful Death,*
this wage of games or speeches, a body leans into

another as a way to get home, and going, there's little
to add up in the heart of the heart of the smoking bar.

Now it is August, now it's a year, and I'm trying to open
the good words to the morning air to somehow calm the need

for elsewhere. It's lunch, easy urges of a cheap motel. Plots,
bills, sweepstakes. A jade plant to Virginia for a lover

who has lost someone. People desire everyday for the wrong
reasons. Are the best wishes possible for more wishes,

the genie's trick, time in a bottle, that hunger rises senseless?
Like or as, sadness and return, this travel of souls picks up

a body of words. You attaches to I, two voices illustrate
where once there were none. Briefly there's a pattern to all

that's undone. Any system's insatiable. It clarifies by burns.
To leave things is to flourish. Our hour of sweat is entrance

to the dance. The black car purrs. The rock star finds an eye.
A waking song in stages. "One, two," it all adds up to takes.

Flesh, our one possession, the heart is its own redress.
Cell of cells, a flower, our passion blooms regardless.

Tiny Tim, a.k.a. Herbert Khaury, died Saturday while singing his trademark song, "Tip-toe Thru the Tulips," at the International Ukulele Festival in Minneapolis. He was a diabetic. Had congestive heart disease too. But he sang in those absurd American flag pants and he meant it. *I remember carnations, white and red, a setting for cannons at school.* "Death is never polite," he crooned in between bites of egg salad. *It was firedrills, Veteran's Day, meeting the Officer, Priest.* Only in America could such a man be a star. I loved him as a kid, his fey freedom. *What does the lyric say? Sweet land of liberty?* I watched him strum his ukulele on Carson, as the furnace rumbled and ticked and my parents settled in under the crazy quilt. Once at a McGovern rally, catching him on TV singing his old sweet song. *Leafletting through the azaleas, the politics of belief, death is never polite.* My father, who had had a few beers, started in with him in that strained falsetto warble. *Tip-toe Thru the Tulips.* Those fat hands strumming, *'tis of thee I sing.* Then my own hands strumming. *Let freedom ring.* Then dancing, dancing, *across vistas or youth, the shining sea,* the Redwood High Patriots' gym floor.

IV.

Today at the office someone
was unkind. I took this
with several grains of salt,
which means I had a mouthful
of rocks. And in my pocket,
a stone, which I let lie.
According to the stone, I win,
but that's just because
a stone has no desire
to make history. For proof,
check the streambed:
the stone's place is long lost
under silt.

IX.

where is its mouth
            its ear

        how many
are there
            here
            in my river

what is its language

can it remember

is it a dead planet

is its name
            a vowel

what might it preach
from a mountain
            of stones

why is this one
            always cold

why
  does it wear me
    from its neck

does God have a stone
        for an eye

XVII.

In a great city
people walk dazed
with stone dust
on their faces.
So much work
to move stones!
But shift them
anywhere; the stones
do not change.
If change is what
you're looking for,
sit cross-legged
on the ground
until it comes.
A stone has no fear
of airplanes—
day by day
their shadows
crawl across it
like a bug.
Look: a building
is falling, just over
your head. For what
do you choose
to be grateful?
And if you have
time to forgive
just one person,
who will it be?

ENGINE WORK: VARIATIONS

I

June morning. Sunlight flashes through the pines.
Blue jays razz and bicker, perch on a fence post
Back of my grandfather's yard. His stripped engines
Clutter the lawn. And everywhere, the taste
Of scuppernongs just moments off the vines,
So sour that you would swear the mind has traced
A pathway through the thicket, swear the past
Comes clear again, picked piecemeal from the dust—.

II

Or else it's late—September—and the shade
Thicker than I recall: those cardinals,
Finches or mockingbirds still haven't made
A sound all afternoon, though ripe fruit swells
On vine, or branch—or bramble. Thus the frayed
Edge of recollection slowly ravels
Away to nothing, until that place is gone
Where the heart would know its object and be known.

III

All right. Not to begin with those back-lit pines,
Those scuppernongs, the jay perched on a branch
Of sweet gum—no, oak, I think. With what, then?
With my grandfather holding a torque wrench
Or ratchet? Some old engine's stammer and whine
Before it starts or doesn't—a house finch,
Singing or silent? Language, too, seems wrong,
Though it's all I have. *Grandfather. Scuppernong.*

IV

To fix him in some moment, word for word,
That man who taught me gears and cylinders, sweat,
Precision of machinery—the hard
Love of assembling things:
      I know the heat

All summer hung like a scrim where pistons fired
And the boy I was watched in the raw sunlight.
Spilled oil rainbowed in its shallow pan.
One birdcall, maybe; fruit on a trellised vine . . .

V

Impossible not to change things, move the words
From here to there. It's late now. Nothing's settled—
Not engine noise nor the sound of one far bird
The mind sings true. Which version of the world
Should I believe? This morning in the yard
Scuppernongs hang and sweeten. Pine boughs yield
Some fragment of the blue jay's call, a sound
The resonant air repeats but cannot mend.

SNAKEBITE

For a moment, hunched in his body's glistening fever,
my grandfather stood rooted to the shade of a water oak
and felt the venom seething inside him. Blear-eyed, he glared
at the dead snake quivering in the cut blades of saw grass
and thought how cottonmouths were known for meanness,
how nothing, not even the precious luck of childhood
could save him, as he stumbled through the weeds
toward the sound of his father's voice, toward
the spiraling heat that rose from the tobacco fields—
and when his father slit his leg with a pocket knife,
my grandfather watched the blood and venom
mix before seeping into the withered roots of brambles.

His father carried him into the sun-blanched barn
and, tilting the can to his lips, forced kerosene
scalding down his throat: the tonic that cured him
within an inch of his life. And though my grandfather
would scarcely recall those three nights he lay
on a soaked mattress dreaming of cottonmouth,
copperhead, the coral's slick rainbow of skin,
when he woke to the tobacco leaves rustling
outside his window, he felt at once his leg's bitten
and blistered flesh, smelled the stench of kerosene
that would always make him think of his father,
of the terrible acts by which love is painstakingly known.

THE HEAVEN OF MEMORY

for John Wood

For example, say the world is nothing more
than this rinse of light in autumn under oak limbs,
the shade-swept brilliance of things
both as they are and as they are remembered,
with those few birds perched on the clothesline
neither mimicking the regal flight of shirts and overalls
nor ferrying the spirit homeward
to the shrill articulations of grief and loss,
but hunkered over the laundry and fallen leaves,
repeating their coarse, discordant syllables.
For the sake of argument, say the starling's wing
is all we shall ever know of the colors
of heaven. Say the soul is a breath made visible
on the cold air, or that the promised end,
like some ripe Miltonic fruit shimmering
on a far branch, tastes of ash before it disappears.
The truth is, no matter how brilliant the logic
of seasons, no matter how sternly we renounce
the harsh God of insomnia and thunder,
something tempts us toward the infinite,
toward a gilded future, embellished from memory:
streets paved brick by brick from the ore
of nostalgia, a photographic silver
where everything we've loved is restored
to its flawed perfection: tart apples
from the tree beside the old house, wisteria
of childhood scenting the hallowed air.
And what if heaven is nothing but desire?
Even so, from that common seed, we cultivate
our thoroughly inhabitable kingdoms.
And the mind, a place of its own, in itself
shapes from the earth its makeshift paradise.

ZAPRUDER

Day off in dark suit & hat,
looking through the view finder
of a new eight millimeter Bell & Howell camera,
paying no mind the open windows, the seizure.
Just how more than half the targets on the grassy knoll
are potential customers, models, women,
how accident & aim could fit them all,
including the car, into frame. It was the sixties,
so before the volume of the motorcade
turned north up Houston then down on Elm,
they passed the camera between them like a joint,
a silent investment. His secretary stood next to him,
confident that their film would change lives,
that what the women wore to greet the president
would influence their sewing machines & needles.
Clicking the power on added something
above & below human to autumn. Now comes history,
that moment when everything begins to wave:
arms, flags, lens, minutes, seconds, silence,
dressmaker, souvenir, evidence.

CARELESS LOVE

In *St. Louis Blues,*
the sound of workers singing
while lifting sacks of feed
moves a young W. C. Handy
beyond his father's wishes
to a street corner jam session,
to The Big Rooster, and Eartha Kitt's
ain't got no friend nowhere lord,
ain't got no friend nowhere lord,
all by myself, no one to love.

Soon he's humming—"Careless Love"—
next to Pearl Bailey who, playing his aunt,
wants to know, "What kind of love
is that?" At the piano, his fingers
dart like promiscuous blackbirds
from key-to-key, winged sinners.

In his father's house
there's no room for earthly love
—one of the reasons Paramount
didn't bother to cast spouses
for father or aunt. When Mahalia Jackson
spots him at The Big Rooster,
he's forced to choose
between music & home.

He moves into a room
on Beale Street where he thinks
of Ruby Dee, his childhood sweetheart.
Royalties from the sheet music
of "Harlem Blues." Nine dollars
& forty cents. "Do you think
this money is evil?"

His voice is satin,
his conk reflects the morning star,
the star of love in eyes,
brown, alive.

Love O love,
careless love.

SLOW FADE TO BLACK

for Thomas Cripps

Like a clothesline of whites
Colored hands couldn't reach,
a thousand souls crossed
promised air and the screen glowed
like something we were supposed
to respect & fear. Daylight
& Sunday were outside,
waiting to segregate darkness
with prejudices of their own.
A silhouette behind a flashlight
led us down an aisle
into The Shadow World,
rows & rows of runaways
awaiting emancipation.
Theater, belly, cave,
ate what got in.
We half dreamt weightlessness,
salvation, freedom, escape.
A resurrection of arms,
we wished were wings,
reached in & out of greasy buckets
picking something the precise
color & weight of cotton.
Just above heads,
Pam Grier & Richard Roundtree
dodged bullets
and survived falls from as high
as heaven—miracles
not worth building
dreams on. And like an ampersand
between eyes & ears,
the soundtrack strung
together images the way
popcorn butter & soda syrup
held us to earth.

LETTER TO MY MOTHER'S MOTHER, ABOUT THE SECOND COMING

How I wish we had not missed each other
so completely—too many months between your leaving
and my coming to even hope we passed
each other in the door. I ask Mama about you
just to hear her say *Oh, you would have loved her,*
How she would have loved you . . .

I know, Mamaw, about Grampa's shotgun and
the iron bedstead, the day you found Mama mute
and sodden in the quilts. I know about the morning
you ran naked through the yard with Mama in
your arms, racing to make it across the tracks,
coal train bearing down, to leave him pacing
mad as fire, on the other side of the rattling cars.

I know the story about a June Sunday
in 1945 when the aurora borealis
slipped down over Mingo County, emerald-green
arcs tinged with red, waving and folding over
Tug River Valley, gathering near the horizon
in a bright, fan-shaped corona. I have imagined you
stepping out of the Armageddon that sweated
and pounded inside the darkened mountain church
into the living green of near evening. You were right,
Mamaw, to expect deliverance sooner
rather than later. *Surely I come quickly,*
Jesus says, the last red words in the Bible.
Oh, I have imagined how it was, the others fearing judgment,
weeping, some on their knees. But not you. Suddenly,
your face is not with the others, you are gone
—half-dancing, half-running,
singing praise, palms and face upturned,
in the way of our people—
up the road to be with Jesus.

There's a boys' line and a girls' line
in Miss Sharp's room, and line leaders.
Three reading groups—Lions, Tigers, and Zebras.

Miss Sharp tells you once,
then it's up to you—Remember what you are.
It's not allowed visiting with your neighbor.

It's not allowed poking your pencil
through your milk carton for the straw,
you get lead poisoning.

It's not allowed telling what you dreamed
for sharing, you have to bring something
people can see. You have to write

with fat pencils that make you
write slower. When you write capital letters,
go almost to the top line, but don't

touch it, it's poison. When it's free time,
you have to use it wisely. When it's recess,
girls hold hands and march

between the tetherballs, teachers, and boys,
and they sing with their faces
pushed out real far—

    We don't stop for nobody
    We don't stop for nobody

A WOMAN IS THE HEART OF A HOME

Some days, the heart wonders how
she ended up in such a responsible position,

moving the blood along and never
going anywhere herself,

never visiting the elbows or going
to see what the toes are doing.

The heart gets a hankering, some days,
for a new sentence to sing,

but an old rhythm thrums
and drums through her rooms,

a bass line, a syntax whose momentum
the heart is hard-pressed to overcome.

The hardest part is, the heart can't stop
even for a minute, wait for a second wind—

Someone will come running, counting
the seconds, pound on her like a door.

And the heart almost always relents,
beats, believes she should, accepts

what she's been told: That of all
the muscles, she is the strongest,

and most involuntary.

RETURN OF THE LOST SON

It is color that carries our lives
out of shadow, all the flesh tones
in a peach. We should learn to handle
each other in this way, like fresh fruit,

like something meant to be beautiful
and nourishing. The father lays his hands on
with this gentleness. He embraces shadows
in the son's clothes. If it were not

for these wrinkles of darkness,
his hands would be lost.
This is the back he knew, the one
that grew and spread in the fields,

like oregano in the garden, thinner now,
every bone countable, but accounted for.
His hands cannot hold the way
he wants them to. When his son, an infant,

slept in his arms even then
his hands were not enough
to hold him with all the joy and ochre
that emerge from shadows,

the golden grip of sunflowers.

DESCENT FROM THE CROSS

Had he been a sack of grain, the fullness
would not have buckled as this man,
purely flesh. Death does not inhabit
the body, it leaves it without intent,

leaves it cumbersome and unwieldy,
and there's no easy way to carry a dead man.
The workmen were all shamed by their clumsiness,
his nudity and the body's lack of humility.

The workman's cheek burned as it braced
against the cooling abdomen
and, while they worked to free him,
a sweet, salty musk from his loins rose,

invaded the workman's nostrils
and he blushed to be so close, to feel
the last warmth leaving the body,
and to know, finally, it all passes

so quietly and into the dirt.
If it weren't for the torchlight, they would look
like robbers in a neighbor's orchard,
ladders leaned to the ghastly trees,

gathering bushels and bagsful of fruit.

TOWARD EVENING AND THE
DAY FAR SPENT

Luke 24:13–32

The two men opened their door for him,
light, smells of hearth-fire entered the street,
but during the moment that he stood
he remembered cutting down trees.

His father had told him, "Stay near me,"
but he wandered into the woods
curious about the darkness and the branches
bowing themselves smooth against one another.

He had been young at the time,
frightened to be in the chest of the forest,
to have it take a breath and then absorb him.
He told the men he would stay, eat with them.

He thought to burn himself out, a brilliant light.
When the men held out their arms
to welcome him, he didn't recognize
a gesture he had learned in the woods

luring swans from water to the shore:
a steady hand, full of seeds, head turned
away not to startle the bird, until only the arm
and the craning neck were between them.

When the food was gone, he turned
and the swan was many times his size,
all wing, all white and flew away.

ADAM'S TONGUE

And here, at last, is what you've all been waiting for,
The tongue of Adam, pink and fleshy, sweet as attar,

Kept behind glass for centuries. And while the world
Raged on it has kept its silent vigil, here chapelled

For all to come and see the first communicant
With God, the Holy Name's first instrument.

What treasure compares to this? Teresa in Avila?
St. Martin's cloak? Or Peter's tongue, with its denials?

And so we have come to keep it here, past the altar
For sacrifice, the stone confessional, the censer

Smoke rising, here ensconced with the bottles of nard
And the monks' hair shirts, and the funeral cards.

Just how it came to be here is not known, but legend
Has it that Cain returned to see his father's end,

Crept in the night to cut out Adam's tongue and carry
It as a token of his fall; perhaps mere story,

But was Cain surprised by the incorruptibility
Of the tongue, its failure to shrivel, blacken to a tiny

Coal-dark flake of soul? This was still body, *father's*,
Live with every spark of care. Holding it, it dithers.

Here it is, the first of blessers, the first of kissers,
The first of namers, the first of acquiescers.

The cost to look is free, but there is a box to donate.
For those of you whose hands, unlike this tongue, aren't mute.

THE LITTLE SPHINX

Luxor Temple

With his semiautomatic machine gun
He waves me over. He's a Tourist Policeman,
But it's still a gun. He leads me through an arch,
Around a corner to some antechamber
Guidebooks don't remember. Arabic
To me is a lizard that darts behind the rocks—
I'll never catch it—and his English is
A mix of McDonald's and *Miami Vice.*
He points to a statue of a sphinx the size
Of a German shepherd, though it's possible
I'm being told to get down on my knees.
But really he is playing the tour guide
And wants me to shoot it with my camera,
And so I do. He smiles. I hand him five
Egyptian pounds baksheesh. He hands me back
My life.
            How American to be afraid.
To make him someone who would kill. Or maybe
It's only human to think we are our own
Most impending danger. We who know
The desert mirage and still walk toward it.
I wonder if the sphinx will bark its question
And make me answer for myself. What are
Two legs at noon good for if not to go
Somewhere else and know that somewhere else?
Though this keeper of an alleyway was tossed
In a corner of a ruined temple, it's still
A kind of crossroads here, two languages
Looking for a way to pass each other
Without first reaching for a sword.
We have done little to quell the sphinx's anger.
He must still want to crack his stone encasement,
Stretch his jaw and tear us savagely.
See the punctures of his canines, how
Like bullet holes, both empty and intrusive.

MY DAUGHTER AS THE ANGEL GABRIEL IN THE *TABLEAU VIVANT* OF VAN GRAP'S *ANNUNCIATION*

I gave birth to an angel, which is wrong
Twice-over, though it's hard to resist the thought.
I neither gave birth to her (just ask my wife)
Nor is she an angel (just ask her rattled teacher).
And yet there she is, in white and wings,
Long lily in one hand, the other held
To Mary as God's proxy. Scrap semantics,
Embrace your sentimentality, I say,
Despite the better angels of my nature.
She is still as she never is at home.
Still enough to be one of the host.
I do not want responsibility
For words, so let my daughter be an angel,
Let the painting live as if a stone was rolled.
It is the ultimate *trompe l'oeil* on stage,
They are there, and they are not, the way
I could pull back the curtain on this sight
To show you all the brushstrokes, that the child
On stage is not my daughter, but may be
An angel yet, one of those who is there
And not there in the corners of our eyes,
Which this little play has meant to fool,
Not out of any malice for the viewer
But to make a world in which I have a daughter,
Because I wish I did, and never will.

LETTER TO MAUREEN FROM TURKEY

Hello friend. Today it was Ankara,
where the women wear cropped tops
and couples drink beer at sidewalk cafés.
That's not what makes me write to you.
At the museum I lingered before a clay fertility goddess
captured in a glass case. She was all
breasts and thighs, all woman,
and there she was, eight thousand years later,
still giving birth, still bearing down
in the way, you'd tell me, women create the world.
Kids are everywhere—everywhere—
in this country. I saw a boy climb the *mimbar*
while his father, praying, touched his forehead
to the ground. Another threw Coke cans in the fountain.
The Ottoman citadel's narrow streets
pulsed with children peddling
scarves embroidered by their mothers
and hand-made lace. A girl named Kemal
held my hand, her fingers fit so easily in mine,
and led me around loose stones
to the top. Paused
above scattered timber roofs and pastel walls,
I could almost trust in stasis, a pristine world.
How did you do it—sign on
for what they call the full catastrophe—
the husband, the children, the solid brick home?
The world isn't pristine, and my trust in it
as flimsy as a cigar-smoking old man's.
You know the type, slumped on a bus,
muttering *What is the world coming to?*
And kids are everywhere.
Did I mention Kemal's eyes were dark like mine?
She wore faded jeans and her haggling, well,
it was refined. In the midst of disillusionment
the world calls for such acts of faith.
You have yours in Amanda and Dan.

I have a new hotel, where neon flashes
outside the window like I'm trapped
in a film noir. Even these travels,
these endless travels, can't be as simple
as Roman ruins and apricots spilling in markets.
The fertility goddess is a postcard
and I couldn't help buying Kemal's lace.

In Prague, where cracked sidewalks are littered
with shit, you offer a ten-foot square of art.
A crowd of people has gathered

around the shapes and curves, rare in this marred
landscape where decades ago spires gave way
to tenements, and hardened

women become part of the towering gray.
They drag themselves and sacks of cabbage,
potatoes, sausage, poppyseed, eggs.

The pavement before you is lavish
with color. Who remembers yellow
during an Eastern European winter awash

in monotony? While change clinks in shallow
buckets, you render the playwright
president in fluent lines, an angel crouched low

on his shoulder whispering words we might
guess at. You step back, ribbons of chalk
confusing your clothes, your creation bright

and animated on the sidewalk
where with each hour it will fade
until all that remains is a mark

in your memory. On a canvas Renoir gave
us a scene—music plays and dancers whirl
while a fair-haired figure bends to savor

conversation. A hundred years later this girl
still bends, still savors, the lace
at her throat still a smudge. But I turn

back to you making art in ephemeral places.
It's true I'll forget the image as transient as sand,
but not the careful debate of your face

or the sweep of the chalk in your hand.

BEETLE ORGY

Bloom up from the earth, blooming and curling
like ribbon, and at semi-regular intervals
sprouting leaves: almost the border art
of a Celtic manuscript, the vines up along the fence
of this old tennis court. Amid the wreck

of the net, the cracks of the surface, the rust
along the poles still standing, the vines
are a saving delicacy. Not jarring at all,
though incongruous—except as a reminder
that the school yard will gladly take this place

back in a few untended years, that between
the vines and grass, the tennis courts
will be ground into meal and digested.
I stop at one of the vine edgings caught
by even finer detail: the leaves themselves

are digested; they have been eaten to
irregular lace, and the perpetrators are still here—
five of them across one particular leaf, lined up
straight and even, like cars in a parking lot.
Beetles: their backs a lustrous green and copper,

taken from the kiln hot, thrown on a bed of saw dust
that burst into flame, then lidded over
so the vacuum could draw the metal oxides
to the surface. At first it looks like there are five,
but now I see that there are seven, no eight—

and that in three of the spaces, beetles
are doubled up, one mounting, back legs
twitching, as if running and getting nowhere;
and one mounted, also moving, slightly rocking
in back, close to the point of intersection—

51

or penetration—in any case, where the bodies
touch. And here I come to it—amid the advancing
vines and decrepit court: they're on other leaves, too,
all around—coupling in company, hundreds of them,
the rows melding to make a single metallic band.

Back in Houston, a friend had parties—
lawn bags in the living room numbered with tape
to store guest clothing; plastic drop cloths
spread out in the spare bedroom (cleared of furniture
for the occasion), a tray of lubricants, different

brands in tubes or bottles, labels black, red, and silver
—a high tea sensibility. The artifacts remained
uncollected in his apartment for days, even weeks
after, when I would drop by to find his talk
transformed, suddenly transcendental—

the communality, he told me, the freedom: not
just from the condom code (HIV negative I
was never invited) but freed of individuation—
nothing less than rapture, men more than brothers,
a generosity of giving and taking, to both give

and take greedily, that he had experienced
nowhere else. Could I understand that?
The room pulsing as if inhabited by
a single animal, caught up in a single sensibility.
Could I understand? I could read transformation

in his face, could see his eyes, feel him trying
to tell me something: to offer this reliable revelation—
what he always knew would come, but what always
in coming disarmed him. As he talked I looked around
the spare bedroom, attempting to see it

in terms other than lust—a couple of dozen men,
how they would have lined up, become a single
working unit on clear plastic, how their bodies
might have formed a neat chain. I looked around
and tried; couldn't I understand that?

So each beetle a tiny scarab, a dime-size jewel
that glints in the sun. I lean over and touch
their backs with the tip of my finger: running
up and down the bright, smooth surface
like piano keys, hard enough to feel resistance

but not to interject foreign music. Together they form
a band of light, a band of glaze, the gold leafing
that shadows the vines in Celtic manuscripts, a living art.
Maybe that's how it was at my friend's parties—
God leaning over the house on a casual tour

of the wreck of the world, noticing ornamentation
where it wasn't expected. Moved to add
His touch, He reaches a hand through the clouds, runs
His finger over the hard arch of their backs, covering
the length of each spine with the tip;

each man brightens at the touch, comes to know
something expected, unexpected, and tenuous—
and God, also, comes to some knowledge
as if for the first time, is distracted and pleased
by the collective brightness of human skin. . . .

Then I think of God fitting the roof back on
my friend's house, and exhaling, satisfied—
just like me as I walk away
from the tennis court, just like the men inside.

BLUE-BLACK

standard poodle. His dog
had a seizure before

I was in the apartment two minutes:
pointed its snout to the ceiling

and froze up, stiffened, emitted
no high, penetrating whine. Just

silence. Later, in bed,
he explained it had been beaten

severely as a pup. But
that it was still a good dog. Nice

to be able to share the intimate details
of his dog's childhood

afterward, our pillow talk. He was
the first man I've ever been with who

faked an orgasm. Or maybe others
faked it better. Not to be

a cad, I asked. He kept his body
to the side and quietly explained that

"there wasn't a lot." "What's with
your dog," I said,

swinging my feet off the bed
to the pile of clothes on the floor, mine

and his. Poodle rescue. He'd hoped
to show the dog, even had

its hair cut right, undignified
for such a serious-looking animal.

You know, once you've had sex
with enough men, you learn to draw

reasonably accurate conclusions; this guy
was molested young. How

do I know that? I laced my boots
while he told me about the time he tried

to show the dog. It was too timid.
Wouldn't even enter the room; all

its training went out the window. Partially
I know by the behavior

he coaxed me into: the scripted
entrances and exits, the cues, props

to appear in one act, to be fitfully
discharged in another. His script:

neither violent nor elegant, but
his pleasure had no part in it. The dog

approached again
after I dressed, laid its black head

on my knee and looked up
with vulnerable eyes.

I cupped its head briefly in my lap
and stroked its ears.

He was out of the room by then
so I spoke to the animal. "You're

a good boy," I said. "A good boy."

COLIN HAMILTON
The Memory Palace (1998)

FROM *THE MEMORY PALACE*

> *"for here there is no place*
> *that does not see you . . ."*
> —Rilke, "Archaic Torso of Apollo"

THE DOORKNOB

extends a hand in greeting.
Like your hand, it's scarred.
When you shake it, you know:
someone with small teeth
has been trying to get out.

THE KITCHEN TABLE

A circle divided in half, like a flat
world with a single river.
This is winter: the river is frozen,
the wood is covered in ice
and there is nothing to eat.
Dust has collected inside the sun,
which hangs from the sky by a cord.
A long time ago, the moon rolled
off the far edge of the world.

is too rough for the couch.
Woolen strands arch out from
its stitch and finger through
your shirt. You'd need
a camel's back, a mule's indifference,
to lie against this bag in peace.
You'd have to fill it instead
with rice or wheat, then open
this room into a mountainy
desert. The only water
would be the small well inside you.

THE ILLUSION OF CHOICE

"And what would you like to be when you grow up?"
"Elsewhere."

Say you could have been raised
by wolves—shrunken, feral,
starving for the last thrash of a rabbit,

or the more calculated ambush of a deer.
Or say the opera had adopted you at birth,
the final aria of a dwindling company

gone bankrupt with passion, your sable
coat the only remnant of their worth.
But no, you chose to be born here, among

towns like Flagler, Bovina, Seibert, Bethune,
places you pass through on your way
to somewhere else, unless you happen

to live here, then you stay,
thinking the name on the water tower
means you, or that oil mixed with rain

in a hubcap is beautiful, which it is
because you own it, or think you do, in your
hand-me-down jacket and the galoshes

you wear for cowboy boots, galloping
along past Hedgecoke's Grocery, Eunice's Cafe,
on your way to face some stranger.

THE LAZARUS METHOD

It's quite an embarrassment,
his lanky frame dragging around
behind you like an ill-seamed quilt,
his skin, the clinging remnants
of a parade that trails him all the way
from the sepulcher as if someday
he might want to follow it back.
Fat chance.
For three days he's been dogging you
like some method worse than death,
saying, "Can't you at least do something
about the *smell*? After all,
I didn't ask for this." And you want to say

that you didn't ask for this, either.
That you were surprised it worked at all,
what with the women howling in your ear
and the lepers outside clamoring
to be cleansed. You want to say
that it was all a mistake, this display
at his expense, that you're sorry
and want to make it up to him.
But you can tell his price

is far beyond atonement,
as his flesh-ragged fingers
pick at your robes, as he says,
"You'll pay for this.
And I'm going to be there to see it."
And suddenly you realize why you've come
to love this man, this stumbling marionette
who still has the capacity for hatred, for revenge.
You want to embrace this failing cadaver
who has promised to follow you
all the way to Golgotha
if he has to.

O - B O N

In sweltering August, on the last night
of o-bon, the three-day festival for the dead,
I arrive in the village of Komagome.
Families sit out at night on their front porches,
drinking tea or sake and tasting sweets,
wearing those cotton robes they slip into
after bathing—bright, loose yukatas.
Doors are left wide: orange paper lanterns
flicker to light the way for the dead,
who are invited to return to their homes.
Tables are set with their favorite foods
and flowers, instruments and books laid out
that they might want to use again.

On the first day the families went to meet
the souls of the dead at the water's edge,
and tonight they will accompany them back.
Everyone is gathered in a small park,
the ground neatly raked. Lanterns hang
from trees and around a small wooden stage,
where women in kimonos dance slowly in a circle
to the music of drum and flute.
One summer I danced the polka
with my mother on a bandstand downtown
at the corner of Main and Water. We galloped
and spun as I held her hand, feeling the back
of the nylon dress she had sewn, white
with a little red and blue somewhere in it.
Here the women lift their arms, appearing
only slightly from sleeves, where
plum blossoms and cranes drop softly away.
They turn their hands like fans and dance alone.

If I could I would find my mother's dress.
I would pick a bouquet of dandelions and place
the soft hearts of artichokes on clean,

60

shiny plates. I would put on the Mamas and the Papas
or Blood, Sweat and Tears; leave by the back door,
the house bright and open behind me,
and down to the river,
curving just beyond our yard,
to meet her at the water's edge.

The conductor's voice
glides over the drowsy heads,
like a familiar hand
smoothing unruly hair.
A schoolgirl in uniform
falls asleep on my shoulder
as the train tilts and sways.
She has forgotten about her satchel,
what she is carrying to school,
and sleeps in this brief lapse
of time before the day begins.
For a moment I have a sister, a child,
someone for whom I must be still.

THE WILLOWS OF GINZA

The willows of Ginza
that ran along the Sumida river
are gone, cleared for wider roads,
replaced by the smaller ginkgo.
Between shorn, concrete banks,
I see a boat coming downstream
in evening, strung with lanterns,
shadows hopping in the yellow
light of paper screens, the rhythm
of drum and wail of samisen strings,
a low chant calling across the water . . .

I remember my mother,
how once I heard her weep.
I am standing in our yard,
holding a branch of willow.
Its little buds will not
twist off easily in my hands,
when I hear her cry,
a sound I've never heard before.
All is silent, as I listen
with oak, the buckeye, and maple.

I am there in the yard,
planted deep for my mother.
I have not gone anywhere.

BLESS ALL THE GIVERS OF PAIN

for Toi

I cannot write a poem to bless all the givers of pain a poem to forgive
those who should not be forgiven a poem to go on forever that starts
with my grandmother who gave birth to my father through pain into
pain my grandmother who loved and hated my father my grand-
mother who gave her only child away my grandmother who told my
father she wished he didn't have nappy hair so he wouldn't be a nigger
my grandmother who ignored my sisters and me my grandmother
who kept pictures of my dark sister and me in her photo album my
grandmother who kept pictures of my fair sister up on her mantle my
grandmother who called me three times in twenty-four years my
grandmother who called me dear my grandmother who died without
telling me she needed me my grandmother who gave birth to my fa-
ther who married my mother whose mother gave birth to her through
pain into pain my grandmother who hated and loved my mother my
grandmother who called my mother black and ugly my grandmother
who called me pretty and brown my grandmother who was ashamed
of my mother my grandmother who was proud of me my grand-
mother who would not believe my mother my grandmother who is
crazy and will not recognize my mother anymore my grandmother
who gave birth to my mother who gave birth to me through pain into
pain my mother who gave me her milk in exchange for my silence my
mother who would not believe me or herself my mother whose words
I hold in my mouth my mother who loved me who loved me who
loved my father who loved my mother who hated my father who hated
my mother who married my father who loved and hated me my father
who gave me his poems through his seed my father whose face is worn
by every man who raped me my father who claims me as his child
when I am no longer his child my father who frightens me when I
don't have to be afraid of him my father who hit me with his hands my
father who held me to his heart that deserved to explode in the pieces
that I keep in my fingers to write this poem for the givers of pain who I
hated who I loved who made me ugly who made me beautiful

TUSCALOOSA: RIVERSONG

for Mister Weaver

1. Black Warrior speaks

The night before they came,
I walked on my river. I had strange
dreams: bloody shouts to the sun,
bodies in the trees, twirling legless.
I sang until morning. I sang, and the white
ones were here sniffing an empty breast.
They are here but I cannot die.
My tribe is strong behind our
drums and sliced trees.
We are strong against these whites
with sticks like dirty breath, these
silly children snatching toys.
They do not see me.
My tongue is strong and hides me.
I cannot die. They do not see me
walking on my river, my teeth biting
at early chains. They only
know they choke on my songs.

2. DeSoto speaks

I have seen him before all
over the world. This Indian,
this Tuscaloosa, this red man
with the black name dares
to think he will defeat me
and my tribe. Who is he to imagine
he will kill me with his songs,
sacred or commonplace?
Who is he to be sure that his spirits
will hear, float down this river,
sting the skin of slaves?
I am the one who cries the music
of God, and Tuscaloosa is mine.
He cannot live past my morning
into night. I want his seed to die

in this water. I want his mouth
wounded with slime.

Tuscaloosa.
I will push him into that river,
this warrior of a cracked womb.
His song will never be earth or flesh.

3.

Tuscaloosa sleeps in the water
stirs the silt of blues
makes music of ashes
feeds death clotted anger

Tuscaloosa sleeps in the water
sucks gore from his lungs
strips the green crucifix
roars the gumbo scream

Tuscaloosa
Tuscaloosa
Tuscaloosa

Trane's *Alabama*
a Creole agony
blood slung through air
a throat-filled epiphany
death licking madness
an elegy for mud

4.

This is the river of no longer.
Here by the side of the Black Warrior,
lights are woven through branches.
Water level signs hang from the trees:
1919 1857 1913 1989 and on.
A memory of what is no longer
painful. From year to year

the levels of the water climb
higher than before, and in the spring
the people of the town visit
mounds filled with bones.
They buy feathers and skin painted
bright colors, or whistles drilled
with holes that make sounds
of animals unnecessary and small.

No one talks of the year he died.
Tuscaloosa is a river, a place
where quiet blood is shed.
Tuscaloosa is a river, signs
nailed to trees. We do not speak
in old tongues. We blow pretty
noises through holes.

5.

Tuscaloosa
This is not the river, so long,
so wide, Hayden's water, baptism
of survival. The river that Mama
and I crossed over one summer,
crossed over history's concrete
back, the river that made her ask,
Do you think we should pray I can't
see the shore this is the river the slaves
had to cross oh God I can't see
the shore do you think we should pray?
This is not Jordan, only the river
DeSoto tossed three hundred souls into,
watched the water grow tall
as they squirmed like dancing
stones, watched the water dark
and struggling rise and rise,
bubbles blowing from the children's
mouths, mother's wet chants
swallowed by dirt.
This is not Jordan.

There is no milk and honey
waiting on the other side, only
dead stones flat and smooth.
This is not Jordan, only simple water
muddied from a season of rain.
This is not Jordan, but I have
prayed at this shore anyway.

6.

Tuscaloosa
feathered with spirit
red libation on the tongue
claws mystery into earth
scatters song on this river

Tuscaloosa
prayer of ancient thirst
wind through clenched fist
claws mystery into earth
scatters song on this river

Tuscaloosa
holy man swept into light
gnarled root of God
claws mystery into earth
scatters song on this river

Tuscaloosa
Tuscaloosa
Tuscaloosa

dark arms cup the blade
blue spit in the scripture's eye
do not walk across my water
do this in remembrance of me

HAREM GIRL

Third wife he made me. Strung me in stone.
Citrine. Amethyst. Smokey Topaz. Garnet.
Third wife. Unheard wife. Hung from a half-gone throat.
Dark and murky one. The semiprecious one.
Unfirst. I am not the one to feel
a phantom limb's pain. The vaporous nothing
of fleshlessness that dreamt of bodying
the bones, that dreamt of most loved and real.
Sister to thin air. I am not a woman
with a lost leg or an amputated
arm that recalls holding him, holding jasmine
oil nights as sole wife, voidless and whole. Removed,
I am the ghost limb that dreamed there
a severed girl and ached for her.

The house opens like a blouse.
This way the windows are jagged stars,
an inward drawn breath.

Draw the house correctly
so that even without them:
   the little mother in her triangle skirt,
   silly sad father in his hat, his mustache,
   the child, the child who holds
   a balloon holds its place
   in the air, a sky punched out
   donut-holed where string binds
   a small stick finger,
we know where they go,
the pathway leading there;
the flowers on their stupid stems,
two leaves will do, five petals
or the serrated teeth of tulips,
three in row, different colors
(make it cheery) wellness is measured
by these things: a doorknob, a chimney
sending smoke signals
to the neighbors about the hearth,
the controlled fire.

Daylight's ended, father's car is drawn
back to the driveway, the mommy draws a sigh,
the child, the child's drawn back indoors.

Black crayon blacks
out the clattering day,
fills the neighborhood
with rest. The riverine
sleepers Z-ing on rectangle
pillows with circle heads.
The moon you must draw
with a benevolent face.
No light must rive the night,
the nightful in their crooked beds.
Draw the covers back and there:

The house opens like a blouse.
The windows are jagged scars.

NEARER VENUS
Letter from the Other Side of the Sky

Ten Years after Her Own Death, the Late Ariadna "Alya" Efron Receives Word That Astronomers Are Naming a Crater on Venus after Her Mother, Marina Tsvetayeva

Oh Marina,

If it's true—as you've said—that the dead are faithful—how will that faith look on you? Like a dress being worn for the first time? Faithlessness being the greater part of Marina, that and your sterling trinkets, and your weathery wheat-colored hair that reeked of wanderlust.

It comes as no surprise that they're naming a crater on Venus after you. A hole on the planet of love and beauty. A planet with a hole in its heart. Your own heart a mesh of lacunae, pitted affection. The planet without satellites. You, too, a planet that could carry no moons.

Loving you was loving that which ached to hold: Broken glass in the pocket. Broken glass in the mouth.

Your friends described you as a mist-wreathed nun, a single naked soul with salty peasant eyes. Grey eyes—the color of ambivalence. A favorite of the faithless. Isn't it? Even I told the biographers when they asked that you were able to subordinate any concerns to those of your work—I insisted *any*—I meant it then as I do now.

Even as child I understood that attachments were too much for you to carry or carry for long. *It was I who once shattered my every happy love*—your words again.

I write to say I *almost* understand: You were down to one loaf of bread, down one daughter, one husband, countless lovers.

Oh Mother of an unrhymed universe, I'm glad a bit of sky bears your name. There are no small craters there, but it is the brightest planet. I wish I'd seen it just once from Earth. From such a beautiful distance it might make sense of everything—might make a lit mobile, bright wind chimes of all those disuniting years I carried long after you floated from the rafters of memory.

FIRST TIME LISTENING TO OPERA

And already I feel my white trash roots erasing,
lodging into the ground
deep as the stem of an unsightly flower.

Already this high culture calls to me;
falsetto dragged from their lungs
like corpses, or stretched like limbs
in ancient torture devices.

How, I wonder, can such urgency
exist in the dark throat,
and spiral down
the huge corkscrew of esophagus?

The intensity, I confess, frightens me;
as if Pavarotti's big head
could flop vibrato strong enough
to swallow daily drudgery;

which makes me wonder
if Puccini could contain himself,
even in the market aisles,
did he slip to his knees

in praise of the fresh produce?
Did he promise
undying love
for each and every endive?
Which makes me wonder
if Maria Callas was ever so moved
she burst into a human vat
of emotional gunpowder,
taking out the trash.

Makes me wonder,
while my lips pulse to the aria
in my small voice, which wants to be heard
no more, but certainly no less,
than their big voices.

PAPER MILL TOWN

So we can have our fine and cherished texts
(those rocket-launched epiphanies emerge
when we scratch temples, eyes hazy in thought),

they went to work—noses upturned in that
nearly shriveled and rotted pulpy stench
tossed sideways into air like chimney smoke

on gray days with no contrast to offer,
every day the same, unyielding; they went to work,
lonely machinists gripped rusty lunch pails

and counted hours, and counted hours,
while the boys—pimply, cactus-stubble-shaved—
pushed mops and daydreamed backseat adventures

with girls who'd never acknowledge them,
and counted hours, and counted hours,
while clippings weighted tile floors like snowstorms

piled high as our shelves flaunting those book spines
on a slight tilt—dominoes that won't drop.
And we lose ourselves in the words, those words,

can't speak the story inside the story,
of how they made thought, and counted hours,
and counted hours—so we can think it.

WE WANT, WE WANT

soon as we're breathing
our baby arms flung sideways
like shooting stars nobody's wished on,
or shipwreck victims, hands raised
up for planes too distant.

We want, we want to be seen,
known by the intricate shift in our voices,
each child's whine a pitch above or
below another's on the grand scale of wanting,
each screech distinct enough to detect our condition.

Which is fickle as a teenage girl
or a faulty compass pressed
to the palm of a sailor's hand, useless.
Because no one can say where anyone's headed,
except toward more wanting.

Wanting someone to note
the mouth's oval of hunger,
the face, and its grimaced frown,
wanting someone to know we've fallen
so in love with our screams we mistake them for songs,

and we conduct in chaos,
each finger-flick like the birth of a planet
we have no maps for.
It's all pandemonium here,
and we're fools to everything but desire,
and the promise that it will always be this way—

always the impossible
terrain between wanting
someone to silence our crying and wanting
someone to pledge to listen to it
endlessly.

REVISING SYLVIA

> *May [Swenson] in the other room:*
> *freckled, in herself, a tough little nut.*
> *I imagined the situation of two lesbians:*
> *the one winning a woman with child*
> *from an apparently happy marriage.*
> *—Sylvia Plath, journal entry,*
> *Yaddo, November, 1959*

Eight-millimeter woman,
phosphoric semaphore
of hands and hair spilling through the projector,
rewind and splice the life
that could have been:

now in your seventies, alive
against a Jugendstil window of Sappho
leaded with pomegranate and grape,
a rich pumpkin soup buttering your lip,
the beach a field of pepper,
white shade, black light
return, return

to Yaddo, leave a hasty note on Ted's pillow
like a bitter mint for him to suck
on his return to the whitewashed studio, the closet
gaping its inaudible white cadence,
your wellingtons in the trunk of a woman
whose fingers will fatten you with poems.

Eight-millimeter woman, four months pregnant,
swelling as the earth shrivels in the frost,
run with your belly full of daughter
and your parcel of carbons.
Flee with the woman who will drive you
beyond this vanishing point

now blurred as the elusive messenger
who hovers, wavers
but refuses to descend.

SHORTWAVE

Warsaw, 1986

From Moscow, London, and Tripoli,
shortwaves winged through the steel V

of our open antenna arms. Shrill dip of a calliope,
your hand on the tuner, then suddenly

the chimes of Big Ben or a Russian
intoning his acquired English like a Californian,

the voice orbiting us beyond the thwack of beaten
rugs, our neighbor's telephone, a violin.

Black-shouldered and square, storied
as a bomber's briefcase, this Grundig 840,

assembled from Czech beer and Cuban lemons,
BBC'ed us kisses of astringent cadence

while we wrung underwear, typed letters,
scraped plates clean after supper.

In January, we slept in sweatpants
and mittens, your warm breath making my hair dance:

for days we lay curled like an enormous ear
listening to concerts, quiz shows, propaganda, war.

I learned in my mother's kitchen, at her hands,
how to whip egg whites cleanly in a bowl,
till they billowed up like a ballerina's skirt,
then dropped like a curtsy on the pie.
I loved to scrape the skin from Jonathans
in curling strips and watch buds of chocolate
sweat saucily, dissolve to glossy waves,
while she supervised, gave orders, held me
to her standards. That's why I prefer it
alone now, no hand on the knife but mine,
my eye sole mistress of delight as I
melt and simmer my way to our repast.
Such priestly offices, chaste discipline!
Sweetheart, I don't want you to watch. You're not
of this order. I, too, have hung around
kitchens of former loves, watching Frank
chop cilantro and chiles, Michael shape
croissants. Like you, I too tried to steal sips,
beg hugs, slip my hand under a belt, but
preoccupied, they bristled with reproof.
Just wait. After I steam the rice, reduce
the sauce, sauté the chicken with tarragon
and grapes, after I watch every morsel
disappear, then, satisfied that you are
satisfied, I'll let you lay hands on me.

THE DESCENT

Finding the entrance is easy, any farmboy
shooting rabbits will sooner or later step
on ground that gives. There's no trick, just keep
going down the jagged slope. Enjoy
descent for its own sake, the narrow pass
that hasn't shifted since death himself took over,
ages ago, the cushion of mud that covers
your tracks. No one above suspects trampled grass.

You must do it alone. The only treachery
comes from hanging rocks and unseen refuse,
harder than stone, left by other lovers.
The river is so pure, you might confuse
it with her song, or soul, or other rivers
that flow between your words and what they signify.

It's colder than you think, down here, the lamp
they strap around your head illuminates
nothing. But a flaming torch ignites
the seeping methane gas and bottom damp,
certain cave-in. And so you must surmise
in darkness how these underworlds operate—
yielding just what's died before a certain date,
say, a million years B.C., claiming only those with ties
still vital to someone above, whose memory
and love sustains.

        My guide lost a father, then
an uncle, when the timbered shafts gave way,
that's why he chugs the train in every day,
reciting to the tiny crowds his story,
returning with neither fuel nor comprehension.

ORPHICS

Each time I write it seems I must descend again,
you'd think it would get easier—finding
the only spot to enter, sweetly demanding
my slow way in. The trouble is what's open

always shifts. One time it's in a brick lace mill
in Fishtown, next between the roots of a thriving
oak, bodies squeezed inside its limbs, almost writhing
like a rodent swallowed by a snake. It's not skill

I need, but perseverance. And the willingness
to fall in love, again and again, with whoever
happens on the scene—someone always does,

and thus, new obstacles, a sort of gatekeeper
who must be soothed and wooed like a mistress,
abandoned only when the slope gets steeper.

AFTER THE RAPE

I

Finally, I wake again
from the dream of giving birth to clay
children and think *Perhaps*
I've already gone mad, for madness
must be this: the tongue's memory
of a tooth where there is only
a sudden gap. I was four, my brother
eight, pulling the wagon, when
it tipped over and my teeth cracked
against warm pavement.
The mind remembers the house
behind the children, but the house
is another thing. The tongue
remembers taste: gravel, blood, sand.

II

When we became lovers I told him
I was folded into thirds,
hidden beneath his body. My body
is no more than its silhouette,
a dark shape under a gauze dress.
I wanted the man to fall
in love with me. But after
weeks of rain everything grows
sick, grows old—even the man, asleep
in a curve of gray
light, is no longer beautiful.
Against the smooth space between
his shoulder blades, my hand feels
the movement of breath through our bodies.

III

I was made of wind, sunlight
or the green translucence of leaves.
Now I am afraid
of almost everything. My lover's
fingers, his eyes, move slowly
over my thigh, over
the curved shadow of my hip.
He traces a line
along my wrist, fragile,
like the neck of an egret.
I was made of water—
a stream, a river or rain.
I still dream of silver vines
circling my ankles, climbing my legs.

IV

Someone says *Did she shower?* Someone
combs your pubic hair, gathers
loose hairs into an envelope. *Evidence.*
They say *Be still* as they photograph
swollen purple bruises on your arms,
your throat, your thighs.
You hear, through a cracked door,
You can't rape the willing.
    Later, collect black spores
from the undersides of a fern's leaves.
On a cord around your neck, carry
a small cloth bag filled with fernseed. Let
the bag's weight rest between your breasts.
This will make you invisible.

V

Don't ask me what moves wind
or how the weight of the moon
bends oceans. I know only
this: I have lived too long

in this body, too often performed
its rituals. Washing: hands
over the rise of a breast, into
the hollow behind the knee.
Later: combing knots
from wet, tangled hair; touching
sandalwood scent on the neck.
This morning I noticed the curve
of a shoulder becoming
the right angle of an elbow.

VI

You can't do anything
but watch as I pull skin
from my fingers. You know
I will touch everything
differently, even your face.
In the dream, I turn
my palms, empty,
toward the night sky.
Love is only this ritual,
pinching open buttons,
tasting skin,
fingers tangled in hair. Hands,
pressed flat to my arched back
might hold us together.

POEM FOR A SON

Someone is here, then not.
You know about things from this.
What holds the world, what goes back.
The flower market, its winding, fragrant aisle
passes on to you the hour someone stood,
stock in love, forever in love, grateful loving you.
Now chicory cries blue.
Now tips of the eastern fir trees lift,
a blanket of stars, a mountainside of candles.
Someone is still standing, loving you.
Everyone you know of,
knows from you a flake of this love.
Yes, water whitens its separations.
Yes, atoms slide through the space of other atoms.
Someone here is yet helping you
load your soul on the bus.
Call when you get there,
someone says. And you call.

In the yard, full bloom
like a brain in flower,
magnificent wig, the tree of it,
the upward thrusts, the dip and rise
of thinking,
of singing that happens
on the surfaces opened toward everything—
you and I, the dogs and Isabel—
her apple-flower hand
held to her ear,
Isabel, full of "Hello?"
looking not as we look at this
tree in wonder
(what we can muster)
but at us, or away, her own way—
And the dogs (not) also looking at the fully laden tree
with its limbs in coatings of flowers,
but also at us or away, from the other side
of human language.
Tree of the brain,
pouring out
what the universe pours in:
I take fifty snapshots, hoping to see
what I see.
I picture its other half,
underground, mirror-imaged
roots forming
the hourglass shape of the whole,
sorting the drift in the soil,
the wellings, a smear of rainsoak—
and the flowers
ridden with the bear-shaped
hunger of bees.

X

My sister who lives in heaven visited last night. She walked figure eights in the living room, dragging a hobbyhorse stick. Her hair was shorter, a surfer girl's. She had a story and, man, she told it. About algebra, and the shape of infinity. Barefoot, she walked to a mountain classroom: math, college. "¾ divided by ½ = X" she wrote on the board. "Look at the X. Where did it come from? Whoever invented X was a genius." Out the door, she pointed to the end of the driveway: morning, a paper in a sheer wrapper folded; the sky attaching by the slender bright edge, the hidden face of the moon.

MOMENTS, CAUSES

> *Modern man has used cause-and-effect as ancient man used*
> *the gods to give order to the Universe. This is not because it was*
> *the truest system, but because it was the most convenient.*
> —Henri Poincaré

Moments arrive like mothers, inevitably
    seamless and charming. History
        is thunder following lightning,

two moments from one cause,
    the seen and then the heard.
        Even the blind, when a light is shone

from a heatless, strangered distance,
    know the silent light's direction:
        up or down—there, there, now.

But wait! When out of time, out of place,
    one particular thing becomes another
        unseemingly: the overlapping

like tops and bottoms of waves that is metaphor.
    What are mothers for,
        if not to teach us to swim

by showing us the motions of arms and legs
    and planets, of flavors and colors, fathers and lovers,
        and holding our young bellies

until we put our faces in the water
    with our breaths held?
        Water, then, is breathtaking,

and we float, suspended
    in we know not what
        until, knowing, we glide.

A THEORY OF FORMATION

They, too, labor,
And if we envy them we should remember
How brief their stay in the ether is.
    "Cumulus," Phillis Levin

Life's the accumulation: the drive
I remember, the sky, the explanation
Of cloud formation I gave you.

Heaping and height, I ranted
With the belief that it matters
To those of us on Earth

Letting *nimbus*
Roll off our tongues
Into the spacious station wagon.

How many hours did you let me
Waste? How could I have known
To envy

Then? I find shapes in those moments
Only now, their brevity lingering
Long enough to miss

And shift. There would be no test,
Nothing beyond my mouthing
The words to you: *alto, stratus.*

The sky curtained God's eyes,
Hid us together, father and daughter,
So that I could explain the universe

And convince you to believe in me.
That's what I have, what suffices:
My trust that you trusted.

Let's barter for love. Isn't a bargain better
than something we'd get for free?

Naturally, we select our reasoned preference
at any given moment. Later, we debate,

become churlish even. Can't the sensible
be sensual?

You give me your family history,
and I'll give you mine.

I offer efficiency, but it comes with
laundry day and multitasking.

You offer the one thing at a time, the reconciling
of a checkbook, the toothbrush to the grout,

but this comes with stacking
of books, bills, everything in view.

I am the out of sight but calendar stricken.
You wear the watch in this house. I keep time.

Exchange theories aren't good with details:
don't count your chickens,

this little piggie went to market, this little piggie had none.
We must think better than yesterday's wants

that we misguessed with good intentions.
Evolution's little luster favors us.

Let's barter every day: why notarize a trade-off,
why not question an even deal,

why not risk a less pecuniary life, bank something?
Love's expensive. Let's haggle.

WAGON HITCHER

I.

I was the wagon hitcher. I raised the tongue
heavy as lead, that you propped on
a field stone to make it
less of a weight. At the right moment
I brought it parallel to the ground
while you putt-putted back. I never
doubted the John Deere wheels—
trusted you like God on the seat, your two feet
on the clutch and brake,
you half-turned to watch,
our bond forged with a satisfying clink
when the pin made the hitch.

Then your callused palm closed around
my little one and you lifted me up to the axle—
your arm hugging me onto the seat
in front of you. And for a few rounds
we two farmers breathed crankcase oil,
grime and sweat, sweet clover and clay
the hum of our harvest.

II.

When you asked for the vise grip,
I brought needle-nosed pliers,
a Phillips screw driver, the wrong size
socket wrench.
The pipe wrench wasn't under the sawhorse where
you said it was. There's no time
for tool school to teach me the mysteries and
where to look for a misplaced crowbar.
Too much goes wrong out here where
a hacksaw hangs till the blade
turns orange in the damp neglect

of a farmer's shop. I'm just the worried
daughter, a poor substitute
for the hired help you need.

III.

How did you fix the broken things—
replace missing mower knives, the sheared pins
and frayed belts? How did we
maintain our distance from the power take off and augers?
Rusty bolts could fly off in your face—
chisel fragments imbed a cornea, welding sparks
ignite loose straw. But we kept our
distance and our wits.
Something kept us out of harm's way,
stopped corn pickers and balers
from eating us.

TWIN SPEAKERS

The Detweiler twins—Bill and Bob—
took over the Calvary Hour Broadcast
when their father died.
"Twin Speakers" they liked to say back
in the infancy of stereo. For decades the
Mennonites listened to them on the car
radio on the way to church. The sermon
before the sermon.

Every time the twins were together
they wore matching suits, shirts, and ties—
even after their hair went white and they
lived in separate states with their blonde wives.
Everyone thought how good it was
that they looked identical. You couldn't
tell them apart.

The day before Bob's daughter married,
he died mowing the lawn. Bill put on
the suit Bob bought for him and
performed the wedding ceremony.
(They always gave you a better deal
if you bought two, he told someone later.)
The undertaker dressed Bob in one suit
and Bill wore the other to the funeral,
next day. For months afterward
he wished the note in the breast pocket
had been from Bob, but it only said

Inspected by #00557. One voice
goes on preaching. The message is
still the same: always about what
you choose, who is saved, and what
happens when you die.

VARNISH

I've waited for a good drying day,
when the air is smooth and flowing,
so I take the sailboat from the barn,
and put it up on trestles near the woods.
The hull I paint red, I'm fourteen,
but the deck and the tiller
and the wooden letters that spell FOX astern
each June I varnish golden.
I say a charm against bugs,
and brush on the varnish slow and even.
It's always morning,
then it's always afternoon,
the day moves as slowly as paint drying.
When two clouds pass
they make the shining varnish ripple
like a river eddying towards the young leaves,
which part. There's a blue avenue there,
flowing to a daytime moon.
I don't know that I'm learning
how to be happy.
I'm young enough to think I'll never
feel this way again.

EYE OF THE NEEDLE

She grows tiny as she grows older,
as if death were a small door
into a child's playhouse.

After her stroke she comes slowly back,
she says, "I can't remember anything,"
so we sit quiet, smiles drifting,

feeling how much talk loves the past.
"It's so hard, getting old.
All I really want to do is sleep."

But faces come out of the dimness.
"I think I've got twenty grandchildren.
Twenty. Why won't He take me now?"

Even without memory she seems exactly
who she was, the triumphant matriarch
still too much a self for God.

So I tell her stories: about her husband
my dead uncle, a wild boy in the thirties,
drinking in Grand Central with my father;

even about the children she's outlived.
The past drifts by us with its tiny figures,
together we try to love the dead.

The women have faces that point
into the black blur of the men,
all dancing in hats. Picasso in 1900
was like Toulouse-Lautrec, but darker.
His dancers live in stillness, caught
as the canvas begins to flatten.
As the vanishing point vanishes
there is suddenly nowhere to dance to,
and the woman who looms into the frame
in front of the lesbian couple
has a strange inward look
as if some new biology has begun.
Her lipstick is tilting, her smile
drifts, she feels the change:
her face will pull apart
and reassemble with more angles,
more noses. The century is turning,
Toulouse-Lautrec will die this year,
and Picasso become the Minotaur.
People in paintings will smile
no longer. It will be the beginning
of the last age, the beginning of us,
torn by the geometries of seeing,
hatless, and not dancing.

DJELLOUL

What kind of name is that?
I invite you to notice *that*
is the sound of deportation.

My name is not contagious.
Is quarantine necessary?
Wouldn't exile be better?

I remember I'm from nowhere
but a spurt in thoughtless dark:
you've nowhere to send me.

It's French, I could say. Who knows
the difference? The difference is that
it's Arabic with French panache.

Jeh-lool, go on, try it.
Terrorists bear the name, scientists
and singers, and a few cashiers

can even say it without help
because they've turned their battlements
into condominia of hope.

    What kind of name is that?
The name of a Saracen lancer
ghosting in the dusk of Provence
and the name of a citizen deported
a thousand times a year.

Stuff the mailboxes and night repositories
against my attempts to insert
flat evidence of my belonging here.

I'm as sick of wanting to get in
as I am of wanting to be heard.
I was born with one of those faces that say

Trust me, you don't want to hear it.
Bad enough listening to myself,
who needs you to confirm the news?

My climate's not suitable for growing
the fruit expected of your tree
and I see you have no patience for experiment.

I've misunderstood great men in useful ways
in the natural course of an alien life,
so why would I quarrel with locked doors?

HASAN IBN AL-SABAH

(Lord of the assassins, 11th century)

Exile is a twofold problem:
no one eludes it and
mourned land disappears.

So while I hoped to complain,
I've nothing to complain about
except the poignant delusion

that some of us belong and
must be vigilant for those
who live among us in disguise.

We need the assassins
to exonerate what we do,
to make it seem less awful.

Hasan ibn al-Sabah lives
in our churches on Sunday,
in mosques and synagogues.

We can't describe his face
because we wear it while
we hunt the foreign devils.

BAMENDA RAINS

I'll never forget the sound—
like forty billion ants feeding
on banana leaves—of rain's
secret armies marching up the valley.

Buckets and floods have turned the roads
to fish ponds, laterite rinks
for the taxis that have no choice
between ruts and stones.

100   Out in the center of Bamenda,
market-*mommies* and hawking boys
duck for cover. They chat and call
under wide zinc eaves. Some use

old and British black umbrellas,
others don immense plastic sacks,
one long side slit open to a monk's hood.
I hear distant massive wind

at the top of eucalyptus trees.
Fog moves in like a cliff, maybe
Mount Cameroon pulled up at night
on huge and silent skids.

Close to, mist blots out everything
save for the goat strangling
under a mango tree,
wound tighter on her tether.

HEARING PAIN

My father's become stumped
by the number "one." On the phone
he can't hear the one word
in the impossible string. A fax,
of all things, to Africa; I've given him

a number he can write
when we go to Cameroon. "In a pinch,"
I explain, meaning "if your heart
should fail, again." In Cameroon
people say, "I hear pain,"

the wracking ache of malaria,
the bone-cracking wounds
that farmers wrap in rags, stooping back
to work their fields. My father says,
"your aunt's had another fall,"

walking the halls at night
in the home. "Yesterday she took off
her dress three times downstairs
before lunch." I know she loves blue.
Perhaps she also revels

in the sound of its rayon rasp
pulled over her head, thrown again
and again, balled up on the floor.
My dad is still talking: "Really,
I feel fine, I just can't hear."

Plunged into a gouged out cave,
I spelunk down this pit to piss, sheepish
amid cocoyam leaves larger

than umbrellas, elephant-ear flat,
and incandescent green. Hollowed
ground's been dug beneath a farm plot,

wet and rooted now with banana stalks.
Sweating men molded mud blocks,
scooped earth from one huge bowl

to build their house. No matter:
women come to plant their farm, crops
aslant in any spare spot fetid with fertility.

I feel five years old, wide-eyed
like a boy caught by *Mommy Water*
at her pool. Gods like to live

submerged in streams; they steal
stray kids, drag them down dank holes,
take them to the bush.

I turn and stare, sudden
and alone behind the compound.
Air like a shut-up house, rank

with sleep, people's din recedes
behind the screen of heat. Normal morning
clamor grows dim and farther off.

READING R. D. LAING'S *THE POLITICS OF EXPERIENCE* BEHIND THE STOREFRONT OF GROUNDS FOR THOUGHT COFFEE

The man across from me labors
through a newspaper. All he knows
of me is a faint smell of cigarettes,
a stare too long for comfort—
and outside, rain. *All men are invisible
to one another.* Since I don't see

people move past, only feel the heat
as shadows swim over me
it means the gilded name arched at the top
of the storefront is not an architrave;
the glass is not a threshold

that can be traversed. *Experience
is man's invisibility to man.*
It means we swim the waters
of our thoughts mute as fish—
currents never crossing. *Experience
used to be called the soul.*

Experience is not confluent,
even though when we move,
me, him, the pedestrians
who can't see past the rain,
we move through each other.

BROADCAST

The news tallies the deaths:
in the burnings of her six children
a woman stands accused of negligence,
for the murder of his fiancé's mother
a man is arrested,
and during the break
rows of synchronized kids in pastels
dance to classic rock on the Gap ad.
Afterwards, the newscasters
are all teeth, speaking
patter like a tongue,
Today is December 4th,
tomorrow will be December 5th,
and so on. We'll spend a lifetime
with these tickers as a spine
as this is transmitted
through space, the static
of some idiot star.

The dumb elephants of memory lumber
across a rocky beach.
Straining into harnesses,
they pull taut the rusty chains
of the anchors they drag.
In this dark
the sky is the land is the sky is
the land. Somewhere in its folds
invisible gulls cry,
drop their hollow-boned bodies
to catch brackish fish.
Every crest of this water
sounds a thousand names
as the waves grate apart on the shore;
however, when the sea absorbs itself,
you hear only yours.

105

ASHBERRIES: LETTERS

1.

Outside, in a country with no word
for *outside,* they cluster on trees,

red bunches. I looked up
ryabina, found *mountain ash.* No

mountains here, just these berries
cradled in yellow leaves.

When I rise, you fall asleep. *We
barely know each other,* you said

on the phone last night. Today, sun brushes
the wall like an empty canvas, voices

from outside drift into this room. I can't
translate—my words, frostbitten

fingers. I tell no one, how your hands
ghost over my back, letters I hold.

2.

Reading children's stories by Tolstoy,
Alyosha traces his index

over the alphabet his mouth so easily
unlocks. Every happy word resembles

every other, every unhappy word's
unhappy in its own way. Like apartments

at dusk. Having taken a different street
from the station, I was lost in minutes.

How to say, where's the street like this,
not this? Keys I'd cut for years coaxed open

no pursed lips. How to say, blind terror?
Sprint, lungburn, useless tongue? How say

thank you, muscular Soviet worker, fading
on billboard, for pointing me the way?

3.

Alyosha and I climbed trees to pick berries, leaves
almost as red. On ladders, we scattered

half on the ground, playing who could get them
down the other's shirt without their knowing.

Morning, the family gone, I ground the berries
to skin, sugared sour juices twice.

Even in tea they burned. In the yard,
leafpiles of fire. Cigarettes between teeth,

the old dvorniks rake, scratch the earth,
try to rid it of some persistent itch.

I turn the dial, it drags my finger back.
When the phone at last connects to you, I hear

only my own voice, crackle of the line.
The rakes scratch. Flames hiss and tower.

4.

This morning, the trees bare. Ashberries
on long black branches. Winter. My teacher

says they sweeten with frost, each snow
a sugar. Each day's dark grows darker,

and streets go still, widen, like ice over lakes,
and words come slow to every chapped mouth,

not just my own, having downed a little vodka
and then some tea. Tomorrow I'll bend down

branches, brittle with cold, pluck what I can't
yet name, then jar the pulp and save the stones.

What to say? Love, I live for the letters
I must wait to open. They bear across

this land, where I find myself at a loss—
each word a wintering seed.

FROM SOKOLNIKY

On Moscow's outskirts, falcon and falconer
once stretched the orbit of trust. They've left
only the name, *sokol'nik,* lost circles from sky
to departed hand. Last orange light

washes through trees tugged by wind. A friend
chops carrots, I slice apples, cramped around the table.
He tells of a strange book—a single word
repeated two hundred pages. (He's forgotten

the word). Reporters crowded, the writer spoke:
"every morning, alone, before light, I'd begin
yearning for the word. As I wrote, I'd lose it,
then find it along the way. At times I'd feel

miles from it, then next to it, then I would hate it
the way you can hate someone you've loved
enough to let go. But it stayed. And here we are."
The sun is lost now, under the blue of new snow.

Somewhere lovers touch tenderly in the dark
as if their bodies were bruised, as if they spoke
different languages. As if they did not know
what days would bring, and they could lose

each other, the thread of a word fluttering
so awkwardly between them. A word
they did not know they already knew, and would
repeat, until even their names were gone.

HOUSE NOISES AT NIGHT

How does the foundation sound as it settles?

No kiss in the tongue and groove, no wrath as plaster
separates from lathe, and here, under these sills, hairline
cracks pretend to be fault lines, portending the eventual
entry of insect, water, rodent, cold.

How cold, how dark is silence?

Plumbing lines, sink drains, vent stacks, cold-water feeds
slowly corrode closed like overindulged arteries:
highways for centipedes and other drivers in the dark.
How deep the insects burrow into cozy-against-the-cold
homes, the sawdust forming into small piles in odd spots.

How ragged is anger?

With the first disappointment, understanding; with the
second, forgiveness; the third, irritation like a burr in
the sock, no sidestepping; with the fourth or four
hundredth, words load like dum-dum bullets: aim, fire.

How true is the algebra of emptiness?

Door awkward as first kisses stick at the jamb, dead bolts
and strike plates misalign, the cold night air burgles
under the door and over the threshold, what swings
squeaks: the divorce of proper closure.

HYPOTHERMIA

Against the soft shoulder, the lover's head.

Against the hand, snow.

Against the warm breast, the baby's wet mouth, the lover's soft hand, the black clothing stretching to the shoulder.

Against the simple pleasure of the soft land, snow.

Against the land, a black house, a warm hand, a lover's pleasure, a bleak cat.

Against the simple, the land pleasures: a simple land lost in snow.

Against soft snow, a lost black cat: shoulder, breast, head, hand.

All reward is virtued. Each episode is a celebration.

The mouse feeds on the hawk. The child's shadow rises.

All the children hum Vivaldi, sit quietly so their teachers can properly instruct, get good grades, abandon arcade games, lock the doors on their peers.

The mailbox is empty. Lies are on the wing.

The well is contaminated with PCBs and other toxic acronyms. The basement is full of water. A child floats like a drowned bird on the waterbed again.

112   All our flights get edited, our itineraries reviewed.

Each bird's another puzzle piece, each child's a part of the cover design.

The crow flies sideways. Phones won't ring.

Pick a card. Nothing up my sleeve. No one at the door. Aces and Eights. Any card. The three of birds.

Watch my hands.

ÉTUDES IN THE NEXT WORLD

Transcription flickers in the tallow light
while this practice room descends to sleep

then yields up just the yellowed bones.
The twentieth century's array of keys

will have to go unhammered now—so many
run-throughs have frozen all my fingers.

This must be territory near the bridge
Bill Evans crosses "Blue in Green,"

just without the lift from Chambers.
How am I supposed to know the changes

to be drawn out of this too-spare music?
Nowhere else to look and I don't recognize a thing.

VICTORY THEATER

for Richard Estes

The marquee almost comes alive when sun
hits the curtain wall that fills our field of vision.
It's punctured like the side of a steamship
with galleries and portholes—a bit derelict,
but true to the velvet palace's original dominion:

comfort and escape. In front, a vinyl garland
of flags announces the apparition of blue skin
that mercilessly shakes inside. At half past six
      the marquee almost comes alive.

Look at 42nd Street's tacked-on sophistication
frozen in the hi-gloss of a summer afternoon.
The painted theater is real as any technicolor epic.
And without a single turning wheel to break the quiet,
you can step back from the curb and see it's 1961.
      The marquee almost comes alive.

Up from the hollow storefronts and caverns
	in cinder block that trapped sounds coming off the river,
some projects stood half-finished, empty halls perfect
	only for smoking, for random persons walking through.
The individuals in question broke wide open in Memphis
	and proceeded unapprehended into myth,
calico dress and Nudie suit streaming through the drowse
	of lights that panned across the interstates.

	•

Some child wasting time, shooting bottle rockets
	from a motel balcony in Winona might not know
a thing about it, but for some there is a pattern in the way
	it all turns out. This system leads our heroine
to the bottom of a bottle, to places where she won't embrace
	the slips of friends who suddenly profess love—
strange confessions made on sofas, abrupt kisses between
	bad silences, all the wrong things once again.

	•

"You're Right, I'm Left, She's Gone"
	bubbled up from under the pavement on Union Avenue.
Those at the source must've shared some misunderstanding,
	some desire to fix their age, and not even wax-faced Jesus
on the dashboard or the smile of an opaque hula girl
	could've kept their wheels from slipping. What a joke
each time the bad luck stories start—no man or woman
	could have made this love go right.

	•

But here they are again, before their fall from Grace.
	Here's love coming live with forty-thousand watts—
why not—*from the Delta to the stratosphere*—
	for those endless clear November nights
when somebody's cut loose for the first time,
	wallet full of twenties, watching for the mileage signs
beside the southbound highway—a road jammed full
	with thoughts of people bound for Memphis.

THE HISTORY OF WOMEN

It was Annie Oakley you wanted, mother.
You said I bore a resemblance.
She rode on my Wild West training cup,
Her round, red sleeves billowing in the wind
As she aimed and fired, astride an indifferent pony.
You called me your own little cowgirl,
As if I could drink in trace levels of her essence,
And grow up a perfect shot.

She never missed. I did.
I called home from a Greyhound station in Oklahoma,
Wounded and pregnant,
Watched my last quarter slide into that cold metal slot
And waited for your answer.
Instead I heard a river of voices,
The static of a thousand conversations,
Like angels repeating the names of the dead.

"This is the story of all of us," I thought,
Picturing Annie Oakley's urgent telegram:
No one boarding the last steam engine West
To her rescue, hatbox in hand,
No one giving her a leg up
Into the red velvet coach,
No one putting a ticket in her gloved palm,
No cucumber sandwiches
In her small room above the saloon.

You said she was part of my blood;
I'd find her deep in my heart;
But that waiting room's full
Of warbrides and mail-order brides,
Runaway teenagers, coal miner's wives,
Seamstresses, suffragettes, secret smokers,
Riveters, writers and waitresses.

They spin like the eggs of a butchered chicken
A spiral around the ovaries,
Tiny and perfectly formed.

Now when you tell my daughter the stories,
It always sounds worse than it was:
Someone voted, someone died, and so on.
A baby is born. A star falls from the sky.

FELLOW TRAVELER

I see you, fetus, feta ball floating in brine;
A bun in the oven, half-baked, still dough in the middle,
Hairless humanoid, safe in your space capsule,
Observing the glow, listening to my heart.
That it is enough for you flatters me.
You dance to the music I make in my sleep,
Audience within the sounding board.
All other voices boom bass, like noisy neighbors
Having a party they haven't invited you to, yet.
You are the next guest to enter the room.
Come, swim in our medium, drink our air!
Come meet the one who's held you for so long.

LAMENT FOR PANGAEA

In the night, Brazil mourns Cameroon.
Longing for the soft fit, before the drift,
Harmonic wholeness, one edge, one wavesong,
Gulfless, the heart's Pangaea.
Wegener, searching the mountains for shells,
Tries to explain:

Gondwana is gone, Laurasia.
Not sunk, no;
Just drifting away, cracking up.
You can call to each other, send waves,
Watch the stars, spawn tiny airplanes,
But never touch again.

In time, you will know a new shape. You will
Swim in oceans warmer than Panthalassa,
Spread to the ends of the earth, and rise
In mountain ranges where once was sea.
You will move on, the strata of another life
Recorded in your coast, a scar to remember it by.

THE VISITOR

Down the hill, in the field of sweet alfalfa, they're
   freezing each other, the children

playing tag and I'm up at the house, I'm
in the picture window, thin
and distant like the glimpse

of a surfacing fish. What dark water
the house is, behind me, settling
into evening. Dusk

and there are, of course, fireflies. Tell me,
what was your name? When you visited once,

by the back road where stones glowed pale
in the moonlight, I was too young, I still thought
I belonged to the world. But now

quartered in this house, watching the neighbors' children
turn to dusk, I feel
I'm ready. Come back

and bring your finest wine, the oldest bottle.
Bring that strange dusty book you were reading.

GARDENING

My mother wants me to look at the agapanthus,
at the trout lily. *Look,* she says
and I look

but I hate it, the garden, all of it

from the sweep of purple violas
seeding themselves like secrets
in the shade

of the poisonous walnuts, to the heavy
stink of the lilies bent over

by the screen door. My mother
says it's labor I mind. But it isn't

labor, the hours weeding in the sun,
because I like monotony. Monotony's

a promise. It's the way she puts her face

into the flower, the way she walks through the garden
without wanting to weep.

My mother doesn't understand why I don't want
    to come home and sit

in the summer house, drinking wine,
watching the sky

abstract itself,

or watch the moonflowers that bloom later, that tremble
    in the dark.

It is always difficult to explain yourself
to the faithful.

THE GERANIUM

How can you stand it—*looking* at things?
   For example, the geranium

out on the patio, the single pink
blossom in the sun? Or stand the sunlight
moving through it,

illuminating, holding the flower open like a high
clear note, an ecstatic
widening

which arrives, arrives. What
do you *do* with it? While the shrubs and the lowest
overhanging leaves

lift slightly in the wind, the blossom

doesn't move. It's the object
of affection, and this is how
it hurts you:

by holding the note open—

Past the front of the apartment, traffic goes by:
one truck, then another

comes on, disappears. And I have

the blossom *in* my vision—
   sunlight, like vision,
making clear the tiniest

hidden veins. I don't know why
I should be here, alive

and having to see this, this bright thing
living in time

or have to see it later, at the end
of the afternoon, when the sun's

lower, its light diagonal across the pot,
    its light then pulling away
across the mossed brick

like a wave, only slower,
slower. The blossom is still pink,
but no longer

brilliant. I'll go back
into the kitchen. But you, are you stronger than I? Can you
    stay in love with it? Make promises,

marry it? Are you so sure
of your position in the world?

STAR-SPANGLED BANNER

"At Talladega you want to wear the red
lipstick, sweetie, red as Satan's tits,"
a well-tanned woman tells her. Already sweat
has soaked the pink bandana around her chest.
Oh God, she asks herself, *how did I*
get here? My agent is so getting a phone call.
Beers bounce from hand to hand and the sky
grumbles with jets. Soon the snarl of cars.
For holy Christ's sake, she sings jazz!
She's not some country floozie, liquored up
and bedding cowboys in her RV. She's got pizzazz.
And soul. No butter-blonde, this girl. She pulls
her red hair down and whips out sparks of red in the sun.
She was born in Texas, and Texas is where she's from.

SOLO FOR LOVERS

She'd like to sing in front of a red curtain,
in its curves the undisclosed crack of the snare
to accent her finger snaps, her outstretched arm,
a little wrist to say you're here to see
her upstage cross and curtsy, not the men
in white suits who flash their brassy bells
with the beat, who bob and sway beneath her,
the little razz that licks up into a swell.
Make no mistake, the world drifts, afloat
on her, the gents with their polite erections,
all those trumpets and drums, their wives flushed
and unspooling while she salts the good places.
You have to take the opportunity, young lovers,
to be that sequined, spotlit girl, to be her.

CRY

"Baby," she sings as if her mouth were full
of bubbles, smooth and round, reflecting light
gently as planets do. It's late at night.
The cymbals rattle and rise, the final push
into the note she pulls from somewhere below
her chest, like a bottle before the stopper's out.
Maybe during the applause a man in the crowd
will whisper, "Baby." Sometimes someone shouts
before she's even in full voice, a cry
that makes her body quiver. A lover makes
a sound like that. So many lovers, the heart
mistakes her music for its own. "Don't you cry,"
she sings, and in the "I" for a moment her voice breaks,
the space between notes where her body pulls apart.

GULAG FUN PARK

On a path in these woods, Lenin stands
thumbless, pointing toward Moscow. In one corner,
he's dressed for winter, long coat and scarf,
head lying sideways at his feet. Ina, I see
you at every tree, ticking your fingertips against
your palm, as if counting out the days
since your mother never returned.

Before a line of trees, Stalin is a bust
bigger than my body, the star on his uniform
bigger than my fanned fingers. Thick coins could fit
into the pupils of his granite eyes. Ina, only
two of him are left; they are armless.

You invite me for tea with broken cups,
used leaves, no sugar. You pace around
your chair, Ina, triple-tapping everything metal.
I tell you of yet another Stalin's chipped face,
the cheek left from a toppled monument,
how, when no one saw, I held it in my hands.

It's easier to talk about the greasy food and cold showers
than solitary confinement, its padded walls stained
with sweat and dirt rubbed from straightjackets.
Or the narrow, ground-floor openings to cells
where prisoners stood naked on ice blocks in winter.
Talk about the cool, rainy city instead of how hot
the execution chamber was, how we sidled
softly in slippers across its glass-encased floor but
still felt as if we were kicking up the dust of graves.
Decide how to explain that we paid to see misery,
to understand how fingernails are strong enough
to scratch names into concrete walls.

RADIATION IN KYIV

Even when cautioned by the radio
to avoid the midday sun, the market women
sweat in it, standing next to umbrellas
that shade their huddled cabbages
and cherries. I pause to worry over
the black mole on an apple.

I think of Chornobyl women, who slept
that night with the windows open,
who sent their children to school,
ankle-deep in radioactive foam
to practice May Day songs.

The radio fuzzed for three days
with no warnings, until the women
packed into lead-windowed buses.
Their silverware would glow alone
for centuries. They return to husbands'
graves only once a year
because buried bones' half-lives can kill.

I stand, blocking other women's carts,
my cheeks already sunburned.
I know nothing of isotopes;
though I know that three reactors
still fire and cool
near the same apple orchards.

MEETING YOU: A DEFINITIVE PLAN

I will not buy two goldfish and name them both Elizabeth Taylor
because there is no telling them apart. I will not decide
they are both Scorpios simply because I am, and because I think
they are mysterious for their distracted way of pouting
around their bowl, turning the curves smoother
each time. Their wet world will not tip like a steaming teapot
into a cup. No cat will lap up its tragic good fortune.
You will not sell me two new fish at a dollar apiece
plus ten more for a new bowl to replace the one gravity got
and you will not miscalculate the sales tax and I will not
not get my change back. Chances are, you will not even work
at Bud's Sea and Sky Shop. So in case that's you shopping
the family planning aisle out of wedlock, don't
let our white-haired family pharmacist
with the spooky, wall-eyed stare catch me smirking
as he assures the woman (who I pray is not your girlfriend)
all the merchandise is "fresh." And since you probably aren't
her supportive older brother checking the date on every box
of every brand don't think to think about some grand plan
passing you by. Tonight I am as simple as the world's last love poem:
I pay for multivitamins, I shoplift a pack of Freshen-Up.
I leave the door swinging behind me, right in front of you.

ACADEMIC AFFAIRS

Why don't you love me, and we can hit the road together,
cruise the lecture circuit and tell other single people

about the work it takes to make it work. Together,
we'll talk talk talk about the necessity of long-term

memory and the value of the grudge. Your flipchart
of my body parceled out like a butcher's map

shows the exact locations of too much and too little
with tiny stuck-on arrows, their sharp points as fine

as my revenge: reading poems instead of lectures,
each one a reminder of other men I left for doing less.

Afterward, alone again, come up beside me, nuzzle my ear
and quote Foucault: *Tomorrow, sex will be good again.*

Now add *But tonight you're on your own.* This is how
itinerant scholars of loss communicate: quote, footnote.

Our end notes and marginalia are full of longing for the pet
projects we can't let go, yours on fixing up my life, mine

a love poem I've been working on for years. It reads,
I can take it if you can; I can take it if you can.

PERSONAL POEM

Be my material! SWF/MFA seeks solution to invention problem. Me: young poet (red/br) well-versed, strong interest in voice. Some cross-genre tendencies. You: scary uncle meets muse. You: literate, but ill-tempered. You: Fickle. You have some major hangups. You is not me. You breaks my heart. I goes on from there.

THE NATIONAL LIBRARY

Sabiha

I had decided to study history at university
the day the library started burning.
I was loaded down with books on my way to my parents' house.

People darted. They jerked like fish
caught on a huge, dry stone.

I stood and watched for the longest time.
Pieces of paper lit on my shoulders and hands.
It was August, my birthday.

I'd been thinking how my mother would cry
when she saw I'd cut my hair. I'd light a cigarette. I'd wait.

I'd been thinking how to tell my father:
History, Papa. Not mathematics. Not physics.
My father mistrusted history.

I stood at the bridge preparing my speech.
The leather straps dug into my shoulders.
I stood until the fish settled on their stone

until ash gathered at my feet,
until it covered my face
and the rest of me.

133

WATER

Denis

Outside, the cement cracks where it wouldn't.
We dig trenches to get to work.
Asphalt on top of asphalt on top of dirt.

I try to go at night, plastic bottles strung like lanterns
around my shoulders and thighs. Which is safer,
the dark walk at night or the sprint in day? It's a running debate.

Sanja thought ahead and filled her closets with water.
Wine bottles, milk jugs everywhere.
We still take them, one at a time.

That's how many she stored.
Much good it did her.
Blown wall. Half oven. Burned, curled wallpaper.

We take one and head to the basement
on days we wouldn't dare run
on nights the cement cracks where it wouldn't.

In the basement, everyone brings different things.
I take a book. Asim takes his makeup.
Mrs. Djurdjić brings her starving Persian.

THE BRIDGE

Vladimir

Between you and me
I sweep the houses clean.
With just this yellow straw,
this one broom. I do it
so the others can move in.

I tell you
the floor of this house is a hundred floors.
This house, I tell you,
is a hundred houses,
more.

To pass the time I watch the broom
rake lines in the dust. I sing songs
or look over their things:

     Pictures, books, children's toys.
No TV sets. No VCRs.
       These were taken first, of course.

And sometimes, between us,
I stop my work and weigh my palm in my palm.

So light.
I think.
What could I have done, one man?

LOVE POEM TO SINISTER MOMENTS

You are the dead swan
floating in the Susquehanna.

The red moon before a storm.
You are the series of scars

on a daughter's arm. The tidy
pool of blood on the 7–11 counter

and the small Asian woman
who wipes it away.

You are, when I'm driving,
the sweet smell that may

or may not be poison
gas spilling over the city.

You are cartoons interrupted
by war, the odd-tasting

drink at last call. You are
the gunshots I mistake

for celebration. Lancaster
cornfields, and behind them,

Three Mile Island, smoking
against purple horizon.

Your confidence astounds me.
You arrive uninvited,

grind glass into the pâte, spit
in the gin, and are gone. I want

your perfect broken backbone
for my own. Your long, thin fingers

that always know exactly
which strings to pull,

which card will send
the house tumbling down.

LOVE POEM TO THE PHRASE *LET'S GET COFFEE*

It's your trickery I love,
your sleek underhandedness,
winking at the start
of so many affairs. I adore
your elegant manners,
one hand on the car door,
the other on the ass.
You don't mess around.
You know the difference
between short and tall,
skim and 2 percent.
You call the shots
in unmistakable code:
chair scraping out,
magazine falling shut,
extra cream, no caffeine,
for the lady. Your designs.
Your calculations. Your one
black eye, winking
through steam at the hand
on the hand on the mug.

INSTINCT

I woke to screaming. Outside, a raccoon
was opening a cat. The cat shrieked like a child
as red ropes spooled from its belly.
There was nothing to do; it couldn't
be saved, was already beginning
to shudder. After another minute,
it was still, its entrails steaming
in the crisp air. The raccoon
waddled away, uninterested.

This is a love poem.
It isn't about the cat or the raccoon.
It's about you, still asleep, breathing
evenly and guiltless, and me, awake
and fascinated. What do you see, sleeping?
Empty hallways, maybe, or broken
bottles, or gardens of flesh blooming
around bullets. You could pull
so many triggers behind your eyes. Or maybe
just a woman, tall, with thin wrists. How easily
I could leave you, slip on my coat and shoes
while you dream of what I can't know. So simple

to kill what we don't understand. But instead
we allow it. We sleep next to each other,
roll over at three a.m. and startle
at the weight that balances our bed. We could
spend a lifetime circling, sniffing each other out,
and then turn to meet a dark, clawed creature
we've never seen but know like we know
our bones. Nothing can alter our course. We are animals
of habit. We shut our bodies down together,
wake each morning gutted and hungry.

SOME CRAZY DANCING

I think I must have spent great chunks of those years
watching the girls and boys on American Bandstand,
the frug and the boogaloo shaking through their furious bodies.
I stood by the TV and danced along. I wish
I could say I was another girl, that my stories were those
of the girl who walked off-set, leading a boy—his license
snug in a back pocket—into shadow. I wish I could say
I was the girl who knew what to do with her tongue.
What I wanted in those years was mostly everything:
The neatly belted torsos, the girl's high tits,
all the worn places on the guy's jeans.
What I wanted was not to have to do one thing.
And in front of that TV as I shimmied, ponied and posed,
one afternoon I heard a man's voice somewhere close by saying
—and this I remember exactly—*Fuck me, fuck baby, do me.*
Of course the voice was inside me. Not hard to imagine why,
but harder to imagine how my own indecency undid me.
I flipped the channel, then shut it off and went out
into a nest of suburban streets; walking past landscaped
lawns, shaped bushes, cut-back flowering trees, the slate
front walks up to doors where anyone might emerge.
I know I believed it was finite:
the universe of sex moving inside me,
stars burning out, streaking through the sky, and me—
too afraid to look up or down. Under a neighbor's dogwood,
under the excitement of petals, I waited for that
insistent voice inside to step out and show me what was what.
I can't help it, it seems sweet now—desire—
can I even call it that?—more a demand,
like Dick Clark calling out some latest dance craze,
some new-fangled routine that you'd believe
might be the season's best.

FOOD

At first there is no blood. At first
there is only the blessed, born naked and blind,
six months fatted on hand-picked grasses, rabbit
that Juan Del Peral is grateful is stupid
like all rabbits and easily lulled into feeling
the plucking of its ears a sign to relax.
Because Juan Del Peral wants to be an honest man,
he picks up the rabbit by its hind legs—
letting its slack body hang—pats it across
the head, pulls the ears until they fall
close to the skull and never turns away
from the others. Let them see, he thinks,
that the man who cleans their cages and sings
to them his best love songs, will strike them down
with not too much effort and less regret. It is true, too,
that the hand that comes down on the soft place
where the ears and neck meet is quick and light,
a lighter hand, for instance, than a man might use
on the body of an erring child. But about regret,
Juan Del Peral is only partways true.
With the rabbit hung to be bled, he sits back
to wet the skinning blade. The rabbits seem jittery.
He thinks how he has watched their twitchy sleep, and how
he has opened a rabbit, held the testicles in his palm before
dropping them in the bucket, how he has pinched
and then pulled back their skin, yanking and
yanking until he wonders if this time
it is his own skin that will go, and how he has bled
the necks, catching the first blood to save for cooking. There,
there, he says to his rabbits,
though he knows that one by stupid one
with short pulls he will convince them of his love
until the ears relax and with a skilled soft rap
he will strike the next beauty down.

MILK

That first winter coming back to our bed what did I want?
My mother tits tongued, licked back to breasts again?
Can I say that sometimes it came on me, a pleasure
in that dark where I rocked, taking the clamp
of the baby's bony ridged gums. How I came back
to our bed one breast overfull and leaking,
the baby fallen off the nipple and into sleep.
I have still not said it—not just pleasure—
a pulse in the cunt in the dark while the baby sucked.
How you slept through the nights. How I wanted that too,
to walk the corridor back and forth between your breath
and the baby's hunger. How it was less walking
than it was prowling, curling around myself
and waking to find myself in different rooms.

How every room that winter was a kind of leaving.
A duct engorged or cracked, without even pleasure sometimes,
a growth spurt so that all day was a frenzy of milk.
I would waste the extra milk into the bathroom sink.
I would look up to see myself in a spray of milk—
some she-beast ready to kill for or kill her young,
or I would not look at myself at all, walking
back through rooms we did not have, waking in moss fields
waking on avenues, sitting on dented car hoods to nurse.
And what of it? What of wanting? What of milk
and the bleaty hunger of this baby and that baby
who have long left the tit? And what of avenues?
What now to say to Jen, who calls
to say she is having the baby no one thinks she should have.
She says she wants to have it and give it up.
I tell her how up in those other days Dick cooked
and ate his wife's after-birth. I was not looking for that.
I was looking for a way back.
I was looking for the mossy tongue.
What of that bed we left there, taking with us
only the idea of the bed, sides we call yours and mine?
I could show you how, even now, I can roll a nipple
and thin drops of clear yellow milky fluid bead
in the folds. I could show you this. Or I could,
as I do, lick it off my finger and it is done.

ON THE CORNER

A woman stands on the corner of Grand Street,
tired and not sure how to get home.
She's not the only one with yellow teeth
or wrinkles around the mouth or memories,
and the sun is descending behind the buildings.
"We're still on the earth! We're on a planet!"
she's laughing and a man passing
thinks she's a lunatic and hugs
his briefcase to his chest.
But it's evening in the city
and little birds are clustering
in what trees there are, clinging
to crowded branches,
their beaks too full of song,
bursting. Suddenly she notices
a certain place where the concrete is cracked,
a familiar mark that always reminds her
of the way very young children draw people
without trunks, limbs sprouting
from big round heads. Now she remembers
where to turn. She's not the only one without
a sense of direction or to whom happiness comes
sometimes like a sharp pain.

143

Sitting in the grass
under the stars
by the extinguished fire,
sitting there after the last trip
with a jug and a pail of water,
amazed at how long the wet logs
continue to sizzle,
mistaking a firefly in the grass
for a spark,
confusing, as I look up,
stars and fireflies,
thinking, though, about my mother,
looking at the brilliant pricks of light
in the dark sky,
at the dark shapes of trees,
darker than the sky they stand up against,
thinking about how much I love
that which is no longer visible,
telling my mother out loud,
not loud, really, but very quietly
saying her name,
the personal name I had for her,
speaking it to the night sky
as our ancestors would
pray to those
who went before
and lit a path back
to the source.

I DON'T MIND

I don't mind so much
first of the month bank lines,
cashing the pale green government check
for a rent money order,
one to pay a bill,
taking the ten dollars left
to Monarch Thrift,
finding a blouse that just needs a little bleach,
new buttons, a wooden puzzle for my son
with only one piece missing.

I don't mind so much
the hot and cranky children
on the food stamp line that winds around the corner,
the girl with heavy blue-black hair
pinned back on one side,
deep dark eyes like wine in a chalice,
her brother beside her,
his finger in his nose,
babies sweating in Pampers,
thighs red with rash,
mothers wiping nipples of dropped bottles on skirts.
It's worth the wait—$88!—
chicken and ice-cream tonight!
And I like pulling my grocery cart to the store,
holding my boy's hand
looking for worms on the sidewalk,
and I like the feel and smell
of the people on the bus.

I don't mind so much anymore
the librarians discovering where I live.
I'm used to the smirking men
who cruise down Ocean Avenue
in white Lincolns with CB antennas,
the family men who don't look in my eyes,
young boys offering reefers and beer.
And I love the potted begonias
in my apartment window,
their fat pink flowers,

the piggy-backs, jades,
the little jelly glass
of phlox and buttercups
pulled from a vacant lot.
If rents go up, we'll have to move again,
but I don't mind too much.

Yet sometimes I pass a little house,
an old one, wooden, white paint peeling, a swing,
grass, spots of dirt,
a broken toy.
I stop and stare
and wonder what it would be like
to have a tree
I'd planted myself and could touch
every morning.
The backs of my thighs
would get to know the feel
of warm smooth wood
as summer after summer
I'd sit on the porch reading to my son
or writing letters.

And if I had a hundred dollars,
I'd buy a bicycle with a baby seat.
We'd ride to Manasquan and Sandy Hook,
but I don't mind too much,
though one day
I was sitting on a grassy riverbank
near the Matawan railroad station
as my son threw small white petals down—
boats for the bugs that walk on water.

It's okay this time,
but this is private property.
The voice was like sandpaper.
I didn't cry till the truck had pulled out.

I held my son and told him
that no one really owns rivers or edges of rivers.
But, still, we can't go back there ever
and I had to look in my young son's face
and say, *yes, this is the way it is,*
this is what I've brought you to.

F. DANIEL RZICZNEK
Cloud Tablets (2006)

RESPONSE ON A CLOUD TABLET

Dear beauty-faced, waiting listener: it pleases me to inform you that I am no longer burning. Not in the swarming wilderness and not in the furnaces of the sea. I have multiplied my leaves, my scales, my hair, creeping out between every atom like a faint wind, which is how I came to witness you pacing alone through the museum, eyes lowered, whispering to the bluer places of your breath. I was preparing to shout when you looked up to the grave eyes of kings, bowls of fruit like fallen planets, silent women on sunlit beds. You must understand I was at that point only a patch of afternoon shade crouching near the courtyard. I have left this up to you. I have now become a pattern that will play in the back of your eye. In case you are wondering, the campaign for reconstruction is humming along like a buzz saw, starting with the space above mountaintops, improving things from there all the way down. If you want to find me, walk out of your door and down the street. You will see a child pretending to cradle a baby against her chest. I will be the air in her arms and you will breathe part of me in without trying.

It doubled somehow in the air of the bathroom, the tomblike tiles and the change, nickels and pennies, shining weirdly at the bottom of the urinal. I pissed on them, Abraham and Thomas, and walked back through the past, the candy. I picked up a pack of gum and saw it again, resting in the empty space my hand moved away from. I thought I wasn't deserving, but there it was in the gaps of the cashier's smile and even her pinky finger, bent like a river over the glass-encased lotto. Every second it adhered to something: patriotic condoms, dead moths clinging to plaster, firewood piled outside the automatic doors. As we sat in the car it reappeared, though not in your rainy eyes or the puzzle piece bones of your ear, but angled in anticipation amid darkening fields: a huge, slow barn, prepared to hold against any wind, any possible buckling from storm, the oldest thing in sight, the strongest for miles.

The rain came in droves. You stood at the window and watched as droplets stacked behind one another, pouring in the light. Only briefly they resembled the movement of a crowd seen at a distance, a throng of mourners. You could not picture then the man who was about to die, twenty miles away, how he hesitated, clutching the railing at the top of the basement stairs and watched for any sign of his grandmother in the water below that seemed to creep up, step over step, as if it possessed legs. You could not imagine him like you did the next afternoon, up to his knees, then his neck, swallowing one gulp of air and going under as you sat stopped at a red light, listening to the clear tonelessness of the broadcaster's voice and watched the formal and unnecessarily elegant waving of the trees, dirty rags tangled in their lower branches from where the waters had risen and touched.

KINDLING

My mother will appear like fire
below the burners, that quick twist
of gas. She will be that blue,
and there will be no turning her down.

Already my skin blisters as I burn
my thumb, watch as the water runs over it,
circles in the sink like her voice, the rush
in my ears, the hot and cold of her words.

Milk hardens in the pan,   151
brown, like my mother's face.
On the outside, the heat holds on,
turns the silver black, forms ridges,

the contours of her hands that curl
around my own until I disappear,
a doorknob beneath her palm,
her fingers listening for some click.

Soon she'll come up the walk,
and the trees will drop their leaves
around her, the yellows and oranges
drifting down among the branches,

sparking as they hit the ground.

OPEN HEART

On your chest the stitches swim,
thin black fish, flesh

like small mouths puckering.
Loose, cut from its wet sac,

your heart cries red
into an awkward gutter where

blood collects like rainwater.
And your ribs, lonesome

and tangled in wire, are a gate
now, swinging open,

letting something in.

UNDERTOW

My mother walks on beaches.
The sand stretches out before her,

gold and worthless.
She thinks the water makes promises

it can't keep, offers waves
like apologies. They fall

at her feet. The air is thick
with salt, the sting in her eyes.

All around her waves rise up
in anger, whitecaps like rows of fists.

3.

What was your world like? A vo-tech major in diesel mechanics,
your hands were always black, the knees of your jeans always torn,
and the soft skin of your face ruddied with cigarette smoke
and the crass laughter of boys who knew just a little more
than me as you rallied in the halls with crumpled pages
of Playboy centerfolds thinking I missed the way you looked
at me in my cheerleading skirt, my arms filled with books.
I have thought more about you in the past ten years
than I could have thought possible in the four we shared
in that gymnasium sweating and cursing and sharing looks
of equal disdain, not thinking about you at all.

6 .

Were you ever in love? The kind of love that makes you wake
with knowing that you are completely gone? I dated the same
boy throughout, a track star immersed in the fear of losing his hair
at an early age. He did all the right things: college-prep classes,
a letter on his jacket, two married and quietly unhappy parents.
You were the one who drove fast cars, drank Jack Daniels
from the bottle in an empty field with a make-shift bonfire
and three of your closest friends and no one noticed
that you didn't come home until two-thirty in the morning.
What girl could love you and protect her reputation?
But that isn't the question, is it? You don't have to be
loved to love.

16.

Why? Or was it your idea to get into the pickup truck,
to sit in the passenger seat and were you laughing?
Our friends said the obligatory things, and I say *our*
friends knowing that you and I did not share the same
company, that we did not even consider ourselves
friends. But there was something there between us,
in the space on the green/black leather of the bus,
in the smile I gave to you easily as thanks
for the slip of onionskin paper I returned, and in the fields
and dirt roads that lined their way between your house and mine,
forming the squares of farms and rounding the disappearing hills
between us.

FIELDS BEYOND FIELDS

1.

Since we lay in the fields beyond the high school,
the boys have returned to claim them. The season
   is beginning. Lights rasp the grass yellow;
the painted stripes shine like skin.
   This is football country. We hold the coach
higher than the clinging hands of corn. We carry him
   off the field. In this town where everyone carries

2.

a gun against the outside, teachers spoke in the quiet
   of nicotine. Chalk clicked like tongues.
Without a pass I walked in halls lit as if by water.
   To stop was to get caught. One hand memorized
the closed mouths of lockers, the gym that crossed
   its streamers like secrets. My fingers passed over metal,
pebbled window glass, door knobs numb against touch, and one,
   unlocked, gave.

3.

We lay in the fields, and I swear to you, nothing happened.
   I was there. I loved him, and nothing
happened. Without our shirts, the ground was cold
   and black, full of living things that moved. I could have
touched him then, in the lightless space
   between two cars on the highway. I could have told him
everything he needed. *To stop is to get caught.*

4.

The beaded heads of the wild sedge must have tugged
at his shirt, and caught in his button holes, a last ragged chance.
   The cicadas were years from waking up and raising
their armored heads in the long grass to die. We lay
   in the fields, our arms a last watch.
The car headlights swept our bodies, skinning us yellow,
   roaming over us like hands, which skim but do not touch.

1.
Hear this:
you are the kind of person
to cup your quiet hands around a moth
or slap it
with the flat of your palm as it paddles
toward the bald GE bulb out on the screen porch.
Because I am your hands
and that light,
that hot dumb light,
burning both our flesh and brown wings.

2.
They say it is a simple operation,
a series of three, really,
performed by a doctor in California.
I could come home pale with a souvenir
blue-veined hospital bracelet
and brand new ear,
so new it glistens,
almost better than birth
and twice as perfect
as the other one.

3.
In grade school, my mother was the art lady.
Every Thursday, corseting her frame
into a shrunken, Alice in Wonderland chair,
she ooed with us over *Blue Boy,* and, to be fair, *Pinkie.*
I felt Van Gogh and I were soul mates.
I would have given him my good ear.
I looked into his blue-walled room and saw my child bed.
Not his eyes, sunken flint.
Not his head, shaved, flinching at itself.
It was my ear
on his face,
my monstrosity in his beautiful pale swirls.
His wholeness destroyed by his own hand.
Mine, malformed by birth, or earlier still.
My deformity is his masterpiece, yet—

4.
They say it is a simple operation.
One, to cut the skin, drill the hole.
Two, to sculpt the bone, make the mold.
Three, to borrow flesh,
steal from my stomach, the back of my legs, perhaps,
somewhere dark where scars will not be seen.
I have only so much skin to stretch.
What if I give and crumble in
on myself? In the end, my body
betrays me and ruins everything.

5.
Who told the pretty girls?
How do they know, beautiful boys
who practice their cruelty on kick balls and the ugly ones?
I should not have swum in the public pool.
I should not have worn my hair in braids.
It is my fault for warming my face in the wind.
But now they know I am devil marked. I am damaged goods.
I am the tattooed man, the leather-skinned snake girl.
Only the side show will take me now,
and the doctor in California.

6.
What did you think,
in those last few moments of normality,
the cool of unsharpened blade,
a razor, I think,
licking the lines of your palm?
Standing in front of the bathroom mirror
did you see how this would look in oil?
Maybe insanity takes care of this,
but no,
I think you knew. Vincent,
I wish I had your power
to cut off perfectness
and hold it out in my hand.
It is a simple operation,
blade into skin, blood onto bone.

THE COMPLEXITY OF ERROR

for Jimmie McCullough, 1951–1959

Someone could explain it now perhaps:
how sometimes we could fling
the rubber ball against the front porch steps
and catch a corner, an almost soundless
kiss so sweet the ball would bounce back,
arcing, like the sun climbs, over
Dad's blue Edsel into Sandwith Avenue
or even over Sandwith, sizzling into
Millie Choma's dewy grass—if we were lucky.

If not, the ball might hit a step slant,
skip against the porch wall,
ricochet against the porch light globe
or screen door until Dad
yelled out, *You God-damned kids*
so loudly he'd start coughing phlegm
and have to light a cigarette.
From an open window in the kitchen Mom
only begged us not to sweat so much.

To sit and still ourselves. And so we did.
And everything was quiet, the air full only
of our nervous calculations. The rubber ball,
red and out of round. A certain angle against
a certain step. The wind direction factored in,
just this or that leg kick, arm speed.
All the necessary other fragments
of the scene, and through
the lower branches of the trees the sun—

the same sun we followed every morning
toward Timken Roller Bearing to MacGregor
School, the same insistent sun
you leapt out for from your father's boat,

one Saturday the summer you turned eight,
and tumbled into Meyer's Lake, your small
shoulders imperfect wings, the wind
too light for lift, the tangle of weeds
you overlooked, still unaccounted for.

Now imagine your life this way: you're still
the same person from the same hometown
with the same parents and siblings, though
perhaps you've Anglicized your family name
or now you're known not by your given
name but by a nickname someone gave you
at the bus stop in first grade. And there
you are—the person you are now except
your memories are different. Just how
they're different doesn't matter really. Say
the house you grew up in is now a darker
or a lighter color or in another part of town. Or else
the bus you rode to school
drove through the countryside past cows and cornfields
under a sky so blue you knew you would remember it
forever. Perhaps the little restaurant
where you never worked is where
you now recall you got your first job and where
you met the skinny boy who would become
your best friend then, despite the time he bloodied
your nose for laughing while the other boys teased him
in the locker room, playing keep-away with his
new jockstrap. In fact, imagine it was this boy who
introduced you to the long-haired girl you took
under the fire escape behind the grammar
school the night before you left for college
and kissed so long and hard you wondered
if you'd live another day with just
your own singular breath to live on. It was
an ordinary night, clear and chilly. Hardly worth
remembering anymore. Except that
when you walk out now
to light a cigarette some autumn nights
and hear the crickets in the grass or smell
the charring firewood throughout your
neighborhood, you want to say, to no one
in particular, half as apology, half as concession:
"Whatever happened happened." And just as
you couldn't have foreseen
who you'd become, you can't now
say for certain who you were so long ago
in those moments that could've gone differently
or could've gone exactly as you think they did.

162

RICHARD TAYSON
The Apprentice of Fever (1998)

AFTER *THE VANISHING*

I didn't know what the movie was about
but I was angry at you for not wanting
health insurance or western
medicine, I phoned 777-FILM
and found the closest theater with a 2:45,
I put on my winter coat and said
"it's your life, not mine, I'm going to a show."
I didn't know it would be about losing
the person you love in the prime
of your life together, I stood
on the corner of Henry and Orange
and heard the voice of Louise Hay,
her meditations you kept playing
over and over until I hoped
she'd become mute in some tragic accident,
I sat down in the dark to forget you.
And then the lovers were in love,
they drove into a tunnel
and ran out of gas,
they argued and she walked
into the fog and he walked
into the sun, and she thought
about dying alone, without anyone
to rock her safely in the cradle
of his arms, he drove
out of the tunnel and found her.
He didn't know that the first loss
was preparation for the big one,
the one you sometimes see in the movies
where the evil person looks sweet,
a man with a broken arm
selling key rings, someone
you could see in a convenience store
and speak with, as she does, leaning
against his car while he shows her
the key ring with her boyfriend's initials

engraved on the front. She gets in
and feels the seat plush as a mother's
breast, he takes the poisoned handkerchief
and covers her mouth, as if with one
deep kiss, at the exact right moment,
and she faints, the way I fainted
the day the doctors told us
you were going to die. Not today
or tomorrow, but soon, and the camera
goes underground, the leading woman
wakes and is not in her lover's arms
or in her own bed, the earth
packed around her tight as her lover's
lips sealing her lips,

she screams, beats her fists
against the coffin's lid, and I don't
wait for the final credits but run
home and open the door, saying
your name over and over, bathroom
to bedroom, and you're there, naked
in bed, silent, not dead, wanting
me to touch you, palm, back,
nipple, mouth, we make love
in the uncaged air.

I DO

I bought the rings at R. J. White Jewelers
from the old man with cataracts
who handed me the black velvet tray,
like a silver tureen reflecting black
orchids at the reception after
we'd kissed. I took
the tray and as I started to shake,
he told me to try one on for size,
then turned his back and blew
dust and dried rose petals
from the mantel. "Been in business
forty years," he said, rubbing
his finger over a smudged
mirror. So I chose the one
with tiny grooves etched
along the edge, I put it on
my ring finger, left hand—what
was I doing, this was not something
I could have planned for
or foretold, once done
it could never be cancelled.
"That's nice," he said, and told me
how he'd opened the shop in 1963,
same location, two hundred thirty dollars
to spare and a love of metals
that alchemized to liquid gold
under fire. "Back then
there weren't too many boys like you
buying rings, no sir. This was
before Stonewall, of course."
It had been years since I was called
a boy, and I thought how I was seven
the day in 1969 those men
in skirts and high heels stood up,
three blocks away, for the lives
of people like me who would one day

walk into a shop and buy a ring
for another man's finger. "You sure
this will fit him," I asked, looking
down at that perfect gold
circle, like a halo that would taste
of fire if I put it on my tongue
and swallowed. He patted my hand,
the way a grandmother would
and said, "If it doesn't, bring him in
and I'll serve the champagne I keep
chilled in back for special occasions."
R. J. winked then, and a white
poodle appeared, as if the dog knew
those syllables of drink by heart,

and I supposed they'd been living there,
together, since 1963, watching the years
go by like the parade passing
down Christopher each fourth
Sunday in June. *Let me not*
to the marriage of true minds
admit impediments, so I gave him
five hundred eighty-six dollars
and held in my hand the velvet case,
soft as my lover's palm, and went
to the Stonewall Bar to pay
my debt of gratitude with two
sips of gin and the feel
of names carved in the countertop:
Michael loves Robert,
Bill + Guillermo forever.
I started to get sentimental,
so I took the F train home and found
him on the couch in his underwear,
I held him for a long time, kissed
his lips and the room crowded close
around us, everyone we loved
took a seat, relatives alive
and dead, friends alive
and dead, everyone who had been
imprisoned for kissing in public,

the ones who were tortured
and had their tongues cut out,
the ones kept in boxes
the size of the body, the ones
tied to a fence and beaten
in the name of God. In front
of them all, I held the hand
of the man I loved
and said I wanted him in my life
for as long as I have my life.
His eyes welled up, and I tasted
salt in the corners of my mouth,
then I tasted his salt inside
my mouth as we
married each other
in front of the Van Wyck Expressway
at 6:15 on June 8th, a Tuesday
which will never repeat itself.

SALT

I want a box with a hinged lid,
a box I can fit my whole hand into.
I want to feel my coarse temper
filtered through fingertips.
Sea. Table. Road. Rock. Kosher.
I want to overdo,
to pucker you,
to make the juices rise
from all over the stove,
drawn to over-seasoned places.
I will raise your blood pressure.
I will carry remnants
in my pockets, surprises
from the twenty pounds I broadcast
melting pockmarks across
our icy driveway. I will follow
you as I do the trucks, forgetting my way,
drawn to the rhythm of the fanning crystals
nicking my bumper, eating my paint.
Take me home before we freeze.
Once inside, I will taste invisible
powder on my tongue and track
your waffled patterns across the hardwood floors.

It's your legs that surprise me most.
Because you're a state of mind, I thought
your head might be your biggest part.
What a bombshell—helmetless,
your wild hair flying as you pedal,
sweat-plastered to your forehead.

You took that slick hill a little quickly.
And I'm not sure it was a smart idea
to ride with no hands.
I lost sight of you around the bend,
imagined finding you
sprawled on the pavement all skinned up.
I used to ride the brakes less;
now, I watch for potholes, skittish squirrels.

Nice bike. Bet it cost you.
That steel frame so retro,
the lugged joints handcrafted,
hand-painted the color of sea foam.
I want to run my hands along the tubing,
feel the spray, touch the hide,
your sweat-stained leather saddle.

DEAR GERTRUDE STEIN

I've been reading Alice's *Autobiography*
and want to say that I too have hic*coughed*
and so could not take my dinner nor say my prayer,
though I think it more likely that I hicc*up*
because it shakes me. I don't know
when I will shake or when it will end,
and so I am not bored. Gertrude,
I have learned the cure for hiccups,
but I will not tell you the remedy
because it is sad to control them.
It involves water and breathing and holding
the nose, but it does not involve swimming.
It may be the housekeeper who startles you
in your Paris apartment, but here it's the lover
who frightened the hiccups from me.
That was before I knew the cure,
and that was better than using the water.
I am not bored with the lover I cannot control,
the lover who surprises the spasms from me.

WILL TOEDTMAN
The Several World (2003)

AT DAWN TAKE HIGHWAY ONE SOUTH
OUT OF TOWN

On a narrow stretch of beach between outcrops
Raised by the force of a tectonic plate
Slipping under the underwater lip
Of this land, solitude is so complete

Only the sandpipers that rush the shore
In search of food when the surf recedes are there
With you to mind its rhythm and survey
The waves. It hardly seems worthwhile, the way

They root for leavings in the tumbling sands
Then scamper back unfed, the frothy tongues
Of breakers after them. Not one pretends
To know a better way of doing things.

There isn't any. They live out their lives
At the water's edge. Back and forth, they test
Its pattern, pace its intervals, believe
Each time the waves have come for them at last.

REPERTOIRE

Evenings when I play from memory,
I close my eyes so I won't watch my hands
Or the hands inside the dark behind the keys.
Around the blanket-dark my eyelids blend
With muted spots of light that pulse and move,
The day goes dark and, unconducted, ends
In perfect slight *ritard,* as if to prove
I couldn't match it if I tried. I don't pretend.
But stitching a seam from dark to dark, I look,
Keep looking, light a candle, and give in.
The room pulses. Lacquer shines, throws back
The slipshod glares, a window. I begin again
And study the hands that follow, play exactly
As I play—exactly—mocking me.

DRIVING HOME

The road is lightless without the light
My headlights bring to it, and sight,
My sight, is a flickering lift and dip

The car mimics on the lip
Of every hill, when with each drop
A tickling in the groin wells up

Just as the air inside the shocks
Expands a bit before they're cocked
With weight again. The car settles

In a trough and climbs to shuttle
Me over another crest. I try
This time to float, begin to fly

In that blind falling where the road
Goes dark and overhanging limbs explode
An instant. You recall the dream:

You slip out an imagined seam
Your body makes around you, sift
Intact through a grate of branches, lifted,

Perhaps, by only lack of heft—
A gift unwrapped. Having left,
I keep driving, and the road

Flattens. Lines extend. I goad
Them into darkness always just
Beyond itself. And the gleam of trust,

Thrown out ahead of me as if
To guard against my wayward drift,
Flickers more the more I try yet stays,

Blackening the dark it keeps at bay.

SPEAKING FOR THE MOON

You cannot comprehend this sky, unblemished
by stars. You cannot know the solemn ease
that settles after an age of pristine night:
no wind, no change, even the dust unstirred
for eons. I have the perfect solitude
of thought (though not what you would recognize
as thought), the choreography of earth
and sun, the dreams (you would not call them dreams)
of oceans. Madmen and lovers fall deranged
without my aid, imagine my waning face
is gazing down in sympathy. But I
am not concerned with this, with human love
or doleful sighs directed at the sky.
The graceful pull of waters, spring and neap,
the ebb and surge of surf over shore—
for these I spend my energies, for them
I wax and wane, seducing the mirrored waves.
It's not what you would recognize as love.

A large coffee and two glazed, hot off the conveyor
and glistening with sugar, cost $2.40.
I'm stirring in cream with a too-short straw,
trying not to burn my fingers, when two Canada geese
saunter past the window. Their curved bodies,
black and gray, balance on graceless feet.
How many vertebrae join in swiveling,
pivoting necks, spelling S, 2, 7, C,
beautiful lines not meant to be read?
The morning commuters steer around them,
easing from the drive-thru, one hand on the wheel,
one holding coffee, all eyes on the geese.
In the parking lot, five more, and the man
who bought a box of crullers says,
"I don't know what those ducks think they're doing,"
and looks like he's never been happier.
My coffee steams through its slotted lid.
We've all never been happier.

The leather case, slim in my palm, could carry lipstick.
Capsaicin stream fires up to six feet,
with marking dye for identification.
One night, here beside the Hebrew College
in Cincinnati, a man ran from behind
and blocked the sidewalk, saying, "Wait!
I want to ask you a question!" I kept walking;
he backed up, still blocking, saying "Wait!"
"What?" I asked, pulling the spray from my pocket,
my thumb poised to slide from safety and shoot.
He held his hands up, fingers spread,
saying "No, no, nevermind," and backed away.
I don't know what he wanted—money, directions?
But this is America, a city, and a woman alone at night.
I would have used it, aimed straight for the eyes,
kept firing until he was on his knees
and kicked him in the head for good measure.

This is the image the manufacturers have dreamed,
or culled from our dreams, photographed
and packaged: a shadowy man hiding
in the bushes, the empty parking lot,
the empty echoing stairwell,
some figment slow and clumsy enough
to be brought down by a pepper spritz.

Real shadows rise up at my side.
No one, the second shadow my own.
Passing a streetlight, another appears; I am three,
I am four, me and all my darkling casts.

white (1997)

MS. DAISY'S CROP

1959. Ms. Daisy opened the door of the home she owned. By 18, she'd been bedded, wedded, and widowed, her youth a fading flower on her Sunday-go-to-meetin' hat. At 25, she stood not much taller than the doorknob. She had thick, black hair, too strong to cut, honey-skin and a coca-cola bottle body. In the daytime she sewed davenport covers in plastic shades and body bags for Death Homes, hands always moving: fast-folding white folks towels, homemade rolls, and flannel winter blankets, in crayola colors. After hours her hands sold white lightnin' in tearoom cups. The young men who came to drink and tried to court, got a polite "no thank you." Once a year she took a week for herself and went somewhere secret. She'd come back with wild hair, a rare laugh, and no details. Time changed to sanctified socials, her daughter's wedding, son's funeral. I saw Ms. Daisy, Samson-hair bowed, kiss his closed right eye. Around 50, she started talking bible to her daughter, God's gift of three score and ten years her favorite topic. At 70, her long hair braided for easier managin', Ms. Daisy began leaving fresh, unbaked bread in the oven for weeks, and her hands missed a stitch or two, but her hair stayed bottle-black. Thanksgiving '94 she invited everybody in the neighborhood to dinner. We showed up in our collage knit sweaters, red leather coats, and high-heel sneakers. "Where's Ms. Daisy?" we asked one-by-one snacking on food packing a lip smacking taste. I found her in the kitchen sitting 80, hush puppy feet and no stockings. Her hair stopped me in the doorway. Short-cropped and silver it framed her face in sterling strands. Her skin honey-folded to wrinkles, she crooked her finger "come here," whispered "last time" in my just-turned 40 ear,—and disappeared.

FUNK

for T. M.

I cling to the funk
want to keep the kitchen in my hair,
suck neckbones 'til they pop,
talk shit with my girlfriends,
eat Alaga syrup and granny's biscuits
with my fingers, smell press 'n curl hair
in a beauty shop on Saturday afternoon,
stand around in my yard sayin' mothafucka this and mothafucka that
laughin' at shit that's funny just because you jivin',
dip in somebody's business
and play the dozens for about a hour,
find somebody who remembers the "signifiyin' monkey,"
go dancin', shakin' my booty and sweatin' until my feet hurt,
and I smell like cheap wine, listen to
B.B. King, Miles, the Funkadelic, and the Temptin' Temptations,
singin' all the words off-key, forget
about everything else 'cept how good it is to be
black.

DIME AFTER DIME

My daughter
tosses a dime in Lake Erie
wishing for her father.

At eleven-years old
she carries around
a brown mailman teddy bear
because at five
that was the last thing
he gave her.

Holding onto secondhand
tears, I flash
to my own wash
without a teddy to cling to
only eyes like hers
and a mama who lied
about my daddy's love.

A sudden hug
catches my arms
twisting to turn
to my daughter
making a wish of my own

tossing an invisible dime.

ALL THE NEEDS

All the little tumblers
near the green pitcher,
the nesting bowls,
the rattle of spoons.
All the mittens lost
behind the radiator,
the rush and return
for what's forgotten—
lunch bag, book, stark
on the kitchen counter.
All the faces too near
the screen, Ed Sullivan,
my father barking,
"Sit back, sit back."
All the blessings,
then the beds,
all the needs left
until morning.
How could there be any secrets?
The clay pinch pots,
the coils of snakes.
All the books with
Scotch-taped pages,
snubbed down crayons,
missing colors.
All the homemade
store-bought clutter,
all the seedlings in the yard.
The endless cycle
of our clothing,
mother folding on the couch.
All the longing
to be older, all
the borrowed,
broken, gone.
The closets,

rifled in anger.
When we were finished,
what was left?
All the diaries
read by flashlight,
the circle dimming,
batteries dead.
All the silhouettes
by nightlight,
the sound of footsteps,
then of sleep.

My brothers never saw the girl
who spied on us through the fence where we played
while the sky dimmed and we grew tired and thirsty
before mother called us in. I'd linger
to be last then looked back to see her
peering at me from between the slats.
Once I heard crying and I went out alone to face her.
She'd snagged her hand on a nail in the fence
and held it to me while I stopped the blood.
I hated her soft sobs, her flattened brown bangs.
Go home, I whispered, as heat lightning bristled
and a warm rain broke in splats along our arms.
Go before they see you. Mother didn't ask
about the small stain at my shirt hem. It purpled
and grayed and I knew she'd probably never ask.
They said I was a liar when you didn't come back.
But you were as real as any loss I could trace
in those shortening days,
faded mouth, pale oxbow, pitiful girl.

It is just a family. I am just a girl
posing at the mirror in a flowered
cotton shift, combing back my short hair,
deciding whether I'm beautiful. I know
the creak in the floor by heart and the hiss
of the door behind me, drawing itself shut.
When I cross the room, my brothers and sisters
don't care, their faces turn to the tv set.
From under the basement stairwell I see
my mother lifting laundry from the dryer,
my oldest brother behind her, white as a sheet.
The *slosh, slosh* of the washer muffles my mother's
words. *Buck up, Buck up,* I hear her warning.
The next of us is about to be born.

EVE ALEXANDRA studied theater at Sarah Lawrence College and creative writing at the University of Pittsburgh. Her book *The Drowned Girl* was selected by C. K. Williams for the 2002 Stan and Tom Wick Poetry Prize. She was featured as an outstanding emerging writer in *The American Poet,* the journal of the Academy of American Poets. Other poems have appeared in *The American Poetry Review, Bayou,* and *The Harvard Review.* Alexandra is currently working on nonfiction and lives with her family in New Haven, Connecticut.

NIN ANDREWS's chapbook, *Any Kind of Excuse,* was published in the Wick Poetry Series in 2003. She is the author of five other books of poems, including *Spontaneous Breasts* (winner of the Pearl Chapbook Contest), *The Book of Orgasms, Sleeping with Houdini,* and *Dear Professor, Do You Live in a Vacuum.* Her next book, *Southern Comfort,* is forthcoming from CavanKerry Press. Andrews's poems and stories have appeared in many literary journals and anthologies, including *Ploughshares, The Paris Review,* and *Best American Poetry.* She is the recipient of two individual artist fellowships from the Ohio Arts Council.

KATHERINE BLACKBIRD (KAT SNIDER BLACKBIRD) is the author of the chapbook *White Sustenance,* published in the Wick Poetry Series in 1994. She received BA and MA degrees from Kent State University, where she now teaches poetry and creative writing and where she received an Outstanding Teaching Award in 2007. Her poems have appeared in *The Kenyon Review, The Midwest Quarterly,* and other journals, and she is an associate editor for the *Arsenic Lobster* poetry journal. Blackbird facilitates writing workshops with children and older adults and is currently writing her doctoral dissertation on the poetics of trauma, silence, and the recovery of voice.

Joe Bonomo's chapbook, *Vanishings from That Neighborhood*, was published in the Wick Poetry Series in 1996. He is the author of *Installations*, a collection of prose poems selected in the 2007 National Poetry Series, and *Sweat: The Story of The Fleshtones, America's Garage Band*. Bonomo's personal essays and prose poems have appeared in many literary journals. He is the recipient of fellowship awards in both prose and poetry from the Illinois Arts Council and lives with poet Amy Newman in DeKalb, Illinois, where he teaches at Northern Illinois University.

Robert Brown has published poems in many literary magazines, including *The Literary Review, Quarterly West, Poetry Northwest, Kansas Quarterly,* and *Cream City Review*. His chapbook, *Sleepwalking with Mayakovsky,* was published in the Wick Poetry Series in 1994. In addition, he has published seventeen children's informational books, numerous short stories, and several scholarly articles. Brown currently lives in Astoria, Oregon, where he also works as a professional photographer, shooting fine art photography for galleries and major stock agencies.

Jeanne Bryner is a graduate of Trumbull Memorial Hospital School of Nursing and Kent State University's Honors College. Her Wick Poetry Series chapbook, *Breathless,* was selected by Maxine Scates and published in 1995, while she was still an undergraduate student. Bryner is a practicing registered nurse and is the author of *Tenderly Lift Me: Nurses Honored, Celebrated and Remembered*. She is also the author of two collections of poetry, *Blind Horse* and *No Matter How Many Windows,* and a book of short stories, *Eclipse*. She has received fellowships from Bucknell University and the Ohio Arts Council and teaches writing workshops in schools, universities, cancer support groups, and elder-care facilities.

Lisa Coffman received the 1995 Stan and Tom Wick Poetry Prize for her book, *Likely,* chosen by Alicia Suskin Ostriker. She has received fellowships for her poetry from the National Endowment for the Arts, the Pew Charitable Trusts, the Pennsylvania Council on the Arts, and Bucknell University. Coffman currently lives in Los Osos, California, and teaches at the California Polytechnic University in San Luis Obispo. She recently completed a second poetry manuscript, "To the Less Obvious Gods."

MATTHEW COOPERMAN's first chapbook, *Surge,* was published in the Wick Poetry Series in 1999. He is the author of two full-length collections, *DaZE* and *A Sacrificial Zinc,* winner of the Lena-Miles Wever Todd Prize from LSU Press, and of the chapbooks, *Still: (to be) Perpetual* and *Words About James.* His recent work has appeared in *Verse, /nor, New American Writing, Chain, The Journal, Pool,* and *Denver Quarterly,* among others. A founding editor of *Quarter After Eight* and current poetry editor of *Colorado Review,* Cooperman teaches poetry at Colorado State University.

KAREN CRAIGO teaches introductory and creative writing at Bowling Green State University, where she also serves as editor-in-chief of the literary journal *Mid-American Review.* In addition to her Wick chapbook *Stone for an Eye,* published in 2004, her poems have appeared in many journals, including *Prairie Schooner, Indiana Review, ACM, Poetry, Crab Orchard Review,* and others. Craigo is a three-time recipient of an individual artist fellowship from the Ohio Arts Council and is a former fellow of the Fine Arts Work Center in Provincetown, Massachusetts.

MORRI CREECH received the 2000 Stan and Tom Wick Poetry Prize for his first book, *Paper Cathedrals,* chosen by Li-Young Lee, and his second book, *Field Knowledge,* won the Anthony Hecht Prize. His poetry has appeared in *Poetry, The New Criterion, The New Republic, The Hudson Review, Crazyhorse, Sewanee Review,* and *Southern Review,* among other journals. Creech has been the recipient of a Ruth Lily Fellowship and individual artist fellowships from the National Endowment for the Arts and the Louisiana Division of the Arts. He currently teaches creative writing at Queens University of Charlotte, North Carolina.

THOMAS SAYERS ELLIS is a cofounder of The Dark Room Collective in Cambridge, Massachusetts. In 2001 his chapbook, *The Genuine Negro Hero,* was published in the Wick Poetry Series. He is also the author of *The Maverick Room,* which won the 2005 John C. Zacharis First Book Award, and is a recipient of a Mrs. Giles Whiting Writers' Award. Ellis's poems have appeared in numerous journals and anthologies, including *Callaloo, Best American Poetry, Grand Street, Tin House, Poetry,* and *The Nation,* and his book, *Breakfast & Black Fist:*

Notes for Black Poets, is forthcoming from the University of Michigan Press. Ellis teaches creative writing at Sarah Lawrence College and in the Lesley University low-residency MFA Program.

DIANE GILLIAM (FISHER) published her first chapbook, *Recipe for Blackberry Cake,* in the Wick Poetry Series in 1999. Her other books are *One of Everything* and *Kettle Bottom,* which was the winner of the Ohioana Library Association Book of the Year in Poetry and of the American Booksellers Association's Book Sense Picks Poetry Top Ten of 2005. Gilliam has also received an individual artist fellowship from the Ohio Arts Council and was the winner of the 2008 Chaffin Award for Appalachian Literature.

STEPHEN FRECH's chapbook, *Toward Evening and the Day Far Spent,* was published in the Wick Poetry Series in 1996. His second book, *If Not for These Wrinkles of Darkness,* won the White Pine Press Poetry Prize and was published in 2001. Frech has been the recipient of the Elliston Poetry Writing Fellowship, the Milton Center Post-Graduate Writing Fellowship, and grants from the Ludwig Vogelstein Foundation and the Illinois Arts Council. He is founder and editor of Oneiros Press, which is a publisher of limited edition, letterpress poetry broadsides. Frech teaches at Millikin University, where he was recently named Hardy Distinguished Professor of English.

JASON GRAY is the author of two chapbooks of poetry, *How to Paint the Savior Dead,* published in the Wick Poetry Series in 2007, and *Adam & Eve Go to the Zoo,* published by Dream Horse Press in 2003. His first full-length book, *Photographing Eden,* was the winner of the Hollis Summers Prize of Ohio University Press in 2008. Gray's poems and reviews have appeared in *Poetry, The American Poetry Review, The Southern Review, Image, The Missouri Review,* and elsewhere. He coedits the online poetry magazine *Unsplendid.*

VIVÉ GRIFFITH's first chapbook, *Weeks in this Country,* was published in the Wick Poetry Series in 2000. She lives in Austin, Texas, where she directs the Free Minds Project—a humanities course for low-income adults in the community—for the University of Texas and teaches creative writing. Her poetry, stories, and essays have appeared in *Black Warrior Review, Gettysburg Review,* and *Oxford American.*

A graduate of the Michener Center for Writers, Griffith is at work on a memoir about retracing her grandmother's 1946 cross-country road trip.

BENJAMIN S. GROSSBERG teaches creative writing and poetry at the University of Hartford. His poems have appeared in many journals and anthologies, including *Paris Review, Southwest Review,* and *The Pushcart Book of Poetry: The Best Poems from the First 30 Years of the Pushcart Prize.* His chapbook, *The Auctioneer Bangs his Gavel,* was published in the Wick Poetry Series in 2006. Grossberg's first full-length book, *Underwater Lengths in a Single Breath,* won the 2005 Snyder Prize of the Ashland Poetry Press and was published in 2007.

COLIN HAMILTON's chapbook, *The Memory Palace,* was published in the Wick Poetry Series in 1998. Hamilton is currently the director of Advancement for Artspace Projects, the nation's leading nonprofit real estate developer for the arts. Hamilton previously served as the executive director of the Friends of the Minneapolis Public Library, where he led private fundraising efforts to complete the new Minneapolis Central Library. His poems and essays have been published in a handful of literary journals, and for the last two years he has been a member of the Graywolf Press Board of Directors.

KATE TEMPLETON FOX (KATE HANCOCK) published her chapbook, *The Lazarus Method,* in the Wick Poetry Series in 1996. Her poems have also appeared in the *New Virginia Review, Green Mountains Review,* and *Crazy River,* among others. Formerly an editor with Ohio University, the Ohio Historical Society, and the Ohioana Library, she is now self-employed as a writer/editor with Textual Healing and lives in Athens, Ohio.

DAVID HASSLER's chapbook, *Sabishi: poems from japan,* was published in the Wick Poetry Series in 1994. He was named Ohio Poet of the Year in 2006 for his second book *Red Kimono, Yellow Barn.* With photographer Gary Harwood, Hassler is the author of the documentary book *Growing Season: The Life of a Migrant Community,* which won the Ohioana Book Award and the Carter G. Woodson Honor Book Award in 2007. He has also coedited two anthologies, *Learning by Heart: Contemporary American Poetry about School* and *After the Bell: Contemporary American Prose about School.* He works as the program and outreach director for the Wick Poetry Center at Kent State University, conducting writing workshops in schools and senior centers.

HONORÉE FANONNE JEFFERS's first book, *The Gospel of Barbecue*, was chosen by Lucille Clifton as the 1999 winner of the Stan and Tom Wick Poetry Prize. She is the author of two additional books of poetry, *Outlandish Blues* and *Red Clay Suite*, the 2006 second-prize winner of the Crab Orchard Open Competition. A fiction writer as well, Jeffers's short stories have appeared in *The Kenyon Review, New England Review,* and *Story Quarterly.* She has received awards and fellowships from the Rona Jaffe Foundation, the MacDowell Colony, and the Bread Loaf Writers' Conference. A native southerner, Jeffers now teaches at the University of Oklahoma.

ARIANA-SOPHIA M. KARTSONIS teaches writing at Columbus College of Art and Design in Ohio. Kartsonis's *Intaglio* was chosen by Eleanor Wilner for the 2005 Stan and Tom Wick Poetry Prize. She has recently completed a second poetry manuscript, "Teatime in Heaven with the Crazy Ladies," and is at work on a new collection, "Aloha Vaudeville Doll," as well as a novel, "The Season of White Flies."

MINDI KIRCHNER received her BA in English from Penn State University in 2002 and her MFA from the Northeast Ohio Master of Fine Arts (NEOMFA) program in 2007. Her chapbook, *Song of the Rest of Us,* was chosen by poet Jim Daniels for the Wick Poetry Series in 2008. Kirchner has also published poems in *Eclipse, Perigee, The Avatar Review,* and other journals. She lives in Youngstown, Ohio, where she teaches English at Youngstown State University.

KAREN KOVACIK is the author of the chapbook *Nixon and I,* published in the Wick Poetry Series in 1998, and of *Beyond the Velvet Curtain,* winner of the 1998 Stan and Tom Wick Poetry Prize chosen by Henry Taylor and published in 1999. Her latest book, *Metropolis Burning,* won the Best Book in Indiana award in 2006. Kovacik is director of Creative Writing at Indiana University–Purdue University Indianapolis. Her awards include a guest fellowship at the University of Wisconsin's Institute for Creative Writing and a Fulbright Research Grant to Poland, where she spent the 2004–5 academic year in Warsaw translating contemporary Polish women's poetry.

LEONARD KRESS's chapbook, *Orphics*, was published in the Wick Poetry Series in 2003. He is the author of two other collections of poetry, *The Centralia Mine Fire* and *Sappho's Apples*. His poems, fiction, and translations from Russian and Polish have been published in many journals, including *The American Poetry Review, Missouri Review, New Letters,* and *Quarterly West*. Kress recently completed a new verse translation of the nineteenth-century Polish Romantic epic *Pan Tadeusz* by Adam Mickiewicz. Kress teaches art history, religion, and creative writing at Owens College in northwest Ohio.

NANCY KUHL's chapbook, *In the Arbor,* was published in the Wick Poetry Series in 1997, and her first full-length collection of poems, *The Wife of the Left Hand,* was published in 2007. She is coeditor of Phylum Press, a small poetry publisher, and is the Associate Curator of the Yale Collection of American Literature at the Beinecke Rare Book and Manuscript Library at Yale University.

TED LARDNER is the author of the chapbook *Tornado,* published in the Wick Poetry Series in 2008. His previous publications include a poetry chapbook, *Passing By a Home Place;* a coauthored composition reader, *Exchanges: Reading and Writing about Consumer Culture;* and a coauthored monograph on race and efficacy in the writing classroom, *African American Literacies Unleashed: Vernacular English and the Composition Classroom.* Lardner's poems have appeared in *Arsenic Lobster, 5 am, Cold Creek Review, Rhino,* and other journals. He is a Hopwood Award winner from the University of Michigan and teaches English at Cleveland State University.

ANNA LEAHY won the 2006 Stan and Tom Wick Poetry Prize for her first full-length book, *Constituents of Matter,* chosen by Alberto Ríos. She is the author of two poetry chapbooks, most recently *Turns About a Point,* and her poems have appeared in many journals, including *Connecticut Review, Crab Orchard Review, The Journal,* and *Nimrod.* She is the editor of *Power and Identity in the Creative Writing Classroom* and publishes widely in the area of pedagogy. Leahy collaborates with an art historian to study ekphrastic poetry and with a librarian to study aviation history. She teaches in the MFA and BFA programs at Chapman University in California.

JOANNE LEHMAN is a poet and freelance writer who lives in Apple Creek, Ohio. Her chapbook, *Morning Song,* was published in the Wick Poetry Series in 2005. She has also published *Kairos, A Novel* and a creative nonfiction work, *Traces of Treasure.* Lehman teaches writing workshops in community programs and is a student in the Ashland University MFA in creative writing program. Her poems and articles have appeared in *Great River Review, Artful Dodge, Kaleidoscope, The Mennonite, Farming Magazine, Mother Earth News,* and in local newspapers and on tourism websites.

ANTHONY LIBBY's chapbook, *The Secret Turning of the Earth,* was published in the Wick Poetry Series in 1995. He is also the author of the poetry collection *Mythologies of Nothing* as well as numerous critical articles on modern poetry and painting in a variety of journals. Now retired from teaching film and creative writing at the Ohio State University, he lives on Cape Cod and is an occasional freelance photographer for the *Cape Cod Times.*

DJELLOUL MARBROOK is the author of *Far from Algiers,* selected for the Stan and Tom Wick Poetry Prize in 2007 by Toi Derricotte. He was born in 1934 in French-ruled Algiers. His mother was an American artist, and he never met his father, a Bedouin from from Bou-Saâda. In his first few months, his mother took him home to New York City, and he has spent the rest of his life in the United States. Marbrook pursued a career in journalism and has worked for the Providence *Journal,* Baltimore *Sun,* and Washington *Star,* among others. He began writing poetry again following the 9/11 terrorist attacks and since then has created a large body of fiction and poetry.

KENT MAYNARD is the author of the chapbook *Sunk Like God Behind the House,* published in the Wick Poetry Series in 2001. His recent poems have appeared in *The MacGuffin, Spoon River Poetry Review,* and *Bellevue Literary Review,* among other journals. An anthropologist, Maynard also works on indigenous medicine among the Kedjom people of Cameroon; his recent prose work includes *Making Kedjom Medicine: A History of Public Health and Well-Being in Cameroon* and an edited book, *Medical Identities: Healing, Well-Being and Personhood.* He is poetry editor for the journal *Anthropology & Humanism* and directs the Honors Program at Denison University in Ohio.

MATT MCBRIDE is the recipient of a Devine Fellowship at Bowling Green State University, where he earned his MFA. His chapbook, *The Space Between Stars,* was published in the Wick Poetry Series in 2007. His work has also appeared in *Cranky, Poet Lore, Alice Blue, Heartlands,* and *Dark Sky Magazine.* Currently, McBride is in his first year as a PhD student at the University of Cincinnati.

PHILIP METRES is a poet and translator whose work has appeared in numerous journals and in *Best American Poetry.* His chapbook, *Primer for Non-Native Speakers,* was published in the Wick Poetry Series in 2004. He is the author of two other poetry chapbooks and the collection *To See the Earth.* Metres has also published *Behind the Lines: War Resistance Poetry on the American Homefront Since 1941* and has translated the work of poets Lev Rubenstein and Sergey Gandlevsky. He teaches literature and creative writing at John Carroll University in Cleveland, Ohio. Were it not for Ellis Island, his last name would be Abourjaili.

ROBERT MILTNER's chapbook, *Against the Simple,* was published in the Wick Poetry Series in 1995. He is the author of six chapbooks and has collaborated on others, including *Rock the Boat, Canyons of Sleep, A Box of Light,* and *Ghost of a Chance.* Miltner coedited *New Paths to Raymond Carver: Essays on His Life, Fiction, and Poetry* and is editor of *The Raymond Carver Review.* His poems, reviews, and stories have appeared in *Artful Dodge, Diagram, Hamilton Stone Review, Mid-American Review, New York Quarterly, Pleiades,* and many other journals. He teaches at the Stark Campus of Kent State University.

JIM MURPHY is the author of the chapbook *The Memphis Sun,* published in the Wick Poetry Series in 2000. His poems have appeared in *Alaska Quarterly Review, Brooklyn Review, Gulf Coast, Painted Bride Quarterly, The Southern Review,* and *TriQuarterly,* among other journals. His first full-length poetry collection, *Heaven Overland,* will be published in 2009. Educated at the University of Missouri-Columbia and the University of Cincinnati, Murphy teaches creative writing at the University of Montevallo, where he also directs the Montevallo Literary Festival.

SUSAN NEALE's chapbook, *The Heart's Pangea,* was selected for the Wick Poetry Series in 1995, the same year she graduated from Ohio State University's MFA program. Since then, she has taught at Augustana College in Illinois and at Capital University. Her work has appeared in *New Virginia Review* and *Richmond Arts Magazine* and has been anthologized in *Table Talk,* a collection of ecumenical poems. She lives in Columbus, Ohio, and has just completed a novel.

KATE NORTHROP is the author of two full-length poetry collections. *Back Through Interruption* was the winner of the 2001 Stan and Tom Wick Poetry Prize chosen by Lynn Emanuel, and *Things are Disappearing Here* was published by Persea Books in 2007. Her poems have recently appeared in *The American Poetry Review, The Massachusetts Review, 32 Poems,* and *Raritan.* She is associate professor of English at the University of Wyoming and lives in Laramie.

KEVIN OBERLIN lives and writes in Cincinnati, Ohio. His sonnet sequence, *Spotlit Girl,* was chosen for the Wick Poetry Series in 2007. His work has appeared recently in *Boxcar Poetry Review, North American Review,* and *Forklift, Ohio.*

MAUREEN PASSMORE earned an MFA from Bowling Green State University, where she received the Distinguished Master's Thesis Award. Passmore's chapbook, *Stranger Truths,* was published in the Wick Poetry Series in 2005. Her poems have appeared in *Sycamore Review* and *The Florida Review* and have won the *Mississippi Review* Poetry Prize. She lives in Pittsburgh, Pennsylvania.

SARAH PERRIER is the author of the chapbook *Just One of Those Things,* published in the Wick Poetry Series in 2003. Other poems have been published in *Sou'wester, The Journal, Pleiades,* and *Best New Poets 2007,* among others. Perrier earned an MFA from George Mason University and a PhD at the University of Cincinnati. She teaches at Point Park University in Pittsburgh, Pennsylvania.

LEE (MCCLEAN) PETERSON's poems have appeared most recently in the anthology *Making Poems: 40 Poems with Commentary by the Poets* and in the journals *Meridians: Feminism, Race and Transnationalism, Borderlands: Texas Poetry Review,* and *The Bellingham Review.* Her first book, *Rooms and Fields: Dramatic Monologues from the War in Bosnia,* was chosen for the Stan and Tom Wick Poetry Prize by Jean Valentine in 2003. Peterson has taught English as a second language at Manhattanville College and held the position of 2004 Emerging Writer-in-Residence at Penn State Altoona, where she continues to teach as a part-time instructor of English and creative writing.

CATHERINE PIERCE's chapbook, *Animals of Habit,* was published in the Wick Poetry Series in 2004. She is also the author of *Famous Last Words,* the winner of the 2008 Saturnalia Books Poetry Prize. Her poems have appeared in *Slate, Ploughshares, Indiana Review, Blackbird, Mid-American Review,* and the anthology *Best New Poets 2007.* She teaches at Mississippi State University.

VICTORIA REDEL's first book of poetry, *Already the World,* was chosen by Gerald Stern for the first Stan and Tom Wick Poetry Prize in 1994. She is the author of two novels, *The Border of Truth* and *Loverboy,* and a collection of short stories, *Where the Road Bottoms Out.* Redel is also the author of a second book of poetry, *Swoon,* published in 2003. She is on the faculty of both Sarah Lawrence College and Columbia University's graduate writing programs.

ANELE RUBIN's *Trying to Speak* won the 2004 Stan and Tom Wick Poetry Prize, chosen by Philip Levine, and received the 2006 Great Lakes Colleges Association's New Writers Award in Poetry. Her poems have been published in *Cottonwood, Midwest Quarterly, O: The Oprah Magazine, River Styx, Bitter Oleander,* and other journals. Rubin has degrees from Louisiana State University and New York University and has worked as a foot messenger, a collator in a print shop, a counter person in a donut shop, a sorter of vintage clothing, a reading tutor for small children, and a high school English teacher. She currently teaches English as an adjunct at Long Island University's Brooklyn Campus.

F. Daniel Rzicznek is the author of the chapbook *Cloud Tablets,* published in the Wick Poetry Series in 2006. His first full-length collection, *Neck of the World,* was chosen by Alice Quinn for the May Swenson Prize of the Utah State University Press in 2007. Rzicznek's individual poems have appeared in numerous literary journals, and he is coeditor of a book of essays on the prose poem (due out in 2010 from Rose Metal Press). He teaches English composition at Bowling Green State University in Ohio.

Mary Ann Samyn's first chapbook, *Rooms by the Sea,* was published in the Wick Poetry Series in 1994. She is the author of three full-length collections, most recently *Purr,* published in 2005; a new book, *Beauty Breaks In,* is forthcoming in 2009. The recipient of a Pushcart Prize and awards from the Poetry Society of America and *Mid-American Review,* Samyn has published her work in *Field, Denver Quarterly, Virginia Quarterly Review, Pleiades,* and other journals. She teaches in the MFA program at West Virginia University, where she is also the Bolton Professor for Teaching and Mentoring.

J. Gabriel Scala received an MFA from Bowling Green State University and a PhD from the University of Mississippi. Her chapbook, *Twenty Questions for Robbie Dunkle,* was published in the Wick Poetry Series in 2004, and her work has also been published in *Northwest Florida Review, Chattahoochee Review, Beacon Street Review, CALYX, Third Coast,* and *Quarter After Eight.* Scala currently teaches English at Lebanon Valley College in Pennsylvania.

Alison Stine's chapbook, *Lot of My Sister,* was published in the Wick Poetry Series in 2001, while she was still an undergraduate student at Denison University in Ohio. Her first full-length book of poems, *Ohio Violence,* won the Vassar Miller Poetry Prize and will be published by the University of North Texas Press in 2009. A former Wallace Stegner Fellow at Stanford University, Stine's poems have appeared in *Paris Review, Poetry, The Kenyon Review,* and other journals. She is working on her first novel.

LOU SUAREZ is the author of three chapbooks, including *Losses of Moment*, published in the Wick Poetry Series in 1995. A Professor Emeritus at Lorain County Community College in Lorain, Ohio, Suarez is also the author of a full-length book of poems, *Ask*, which won the First Series Award from Mid-List Press.

RICHARD TAYSON has published two books with the Wick Poetry Series of the Kent State University Press. His first book, *The Apprentice of Fever*, won the Stan and Tom Wick Poetry Prize chosen by Marilyn Hacker in 1997. His second book of poetry, *The World Underneath*, was published in 2008. Tayson's awards include a New York Foundation for the Arts Fellowship and a Pushcart Prize. His poems, articles, and reviews have appeared in *Paris Review, Virginia Quarterly Review, The Kenyon Review, The Advocate*, and many other journals. Tayson has taught at Rutgers University, City University of New York, and The New School. He is currently a Chancellors Fellow in the PhD program in English at City University of New York's Graduate Center.

LIZ TILTON earned a BS from Miami University and an MA and a PhD in English literature from the University of Cincinnati. Tilton's first chapbook, *Salt*, was published in the Wick Poetry Series in 2009. Her poems have appeared in *Southern Review, Southern Humanities Review, Valparaiso Poetry Review, JAMA (Journal of the American Medical Association)*, and elsewhere. Currently, Tilton is writing a history of Cincinnati's Findlay Market, Ohio's oldest public market in continuous operation. She works at the University of Cincinnati's Center for the Enhancement of Teaching & Learning.

WILL TOEDTMAN's chapbook, *The Several World*, was published in the Wick Poetry Series in 2003. He holds an MFA from Johns Hopkins University and lives in Cincinnati, Ohio, where he works as a musician and music teacher.

JULIANA GRAY (VICE) is an assistant professor of English at Alfred University in western New York. Her chapbook, *History in Bones*, was published in the Wick Poetry Series in 2001. She also published a full-length collection, *The Man Under My Skin*, in 2005. Her poems have been featured in Ted Kooser's "American Life in Poetry" column, and she has been nominated twice for the Pushcart Prize. Since 2000, she has taught a summer workshop at the Sewanee Young Writers' Conference and worked on the staff of the Sewanee Writers' Conference.

MARY E. WEEMS published her chapbook, *white,* in the Wick Poetry Series in 1997. She is the author of several other chapbooks, including *Tampon Class,* published in 2005. Weems has published widely on the imagination-intellect as the primary goal of public education and is the author of *Public Education and the Imagination-Intellect: I Speak from the Wound in My Mouth.* She currently teaches in the Department of Education and Allied Studies at John Carroll University in Cleveland, Ohio, and works as a language-artist-scholar in schools and universities. Her new book of poems, *An Unmistakable Shade of Red and the Obama Chronicles,* is forthcoming from Bottom Dog Press.

ROSEMARY WILLEY is a freelance writer and teacher in Kalamazoo, Michigan. Her first book, *Intended Place,* was chosen by Yusef Komunyakaa as the winner of the 1996 Stan and Tom Wick Poetry Prize. Her poems have appeared in *Poetry, Ploughshares, Indiana Review, Crazy-horse,* and other journals. She teaches writing classes at the Montessori School in Kalamazoo, where she heads the Kalamazoo-Pushkin Elementary Poetry Exchange Project. She is currently completing her second book of poems and has also recorded *Farther Down the Line,* a CD of original folk music in which she sings accompanied by her three brothers.